Telling the Story of the Local Church

Telling the Story of the Local Church

The Who, What, When, Where and Why of Communication

Velma Sumrall

Lucille Germany

A Crossroad Book • The Seabury Press • New York

1979
The Seabury Press
815 Second Avenue
New York, N.Y. 10017

Printed in the United States of America

Library of Congress Cataloging in Publication Data

Sumrall, Velma, 1927-
Telling the story of the local church.
"A Crossroad book."
1. Church publicity. 2. Mass media in religion.
I. Germany, Lucille, joint author. II. Title.
BV653.S92 1979   254.4   79-3934   ISBN 0-8164-2193-5

Contents

Introduction

Mankind has become one, comments author Alexander Solzhenitsyn in an acceptance speech he prepared for the Nobel Prize but never delivered. "Not steadfastly one as communities or nations used to be, not united through years of mutual experience, not through possession of a single eye or a common native language but, surpassing all barriers, through international broadcasting and printing."

Mass communication has become a global arena in which many struggle to be a single overpowering voice. The late Abraham Joshua Heschel, Jewish theologian and teacher, could have been describing that arena when he told an interfaith audience, "The spirit is a still small voice, and the masters of vulgarity use loudspeakers."

So it is reluctantly that the church enters the media arena, somewhat as an uncomfortable child exhibiting guilt feelings for being where it somehow feels it should not be. And there is the mistaken apprehension that the Gospel will make itself known somehow without the church. Evangelism, the promulgation of the message of the church, then, is largely a matter of one-to-one communication with the old tools, the sermon, the Sunday School, the cottage meeting the prayer group.

In mass communication there is a faithful audience for what millions believe to be the greatest story ever told in the Gospel of our Lord Jesus Christ, the essential of man's freedom to live and love beyond the boundaries of himself. If we confine ourselves to retelling a 2,000 year old story, if we limit ourselves to a one-to-one posture, are we communicating what we really know of that Gospel?

Historically, the church has been a creative body, firing the imaginations of men to use their genius in bringing the message of Christ to the world. The paintbrush, the fresco, the canvas, the illuminated script were embraced as tools for that expression by both those who "wore the cloth" and those whose ordination came through inner conviction only.

Using the tools that are before us—films and tapes, high speed presses and lithography, television, radio, newspapers, flyers, leaflets, mailouts—let us be faithful to our convictions. We have a responsibility that transcends publicity, promotion, or public relations.

What greater service can the church perform in its mission than to articulate the Gospel in the midst of a complex society in ways in which it can be heard, not always liked, not always accepted, certainly not always followed, but *there*.

If we are to communicate the Gospel in many and myriad shapes and forms, we must grab hold of the instruments of technology and take charge, as surely as Moses, on God's command, picked up the rod to lead God's people from bondage. We have become paralyzed (and enslaved) by the very instruments we have helped to create; and we are bound by our unwillingness to act upon our convictions.

It is not the task of communications to create what is not there but to convey what is there, creatively. We offer the suggestions in this book as a means of communicating the church today, however imperfectly, however incomplete. The Book of Proverbs advises us that without a vision, a people perish. Communications gives expression to that vision, a part of the now and a part of the tomorrow. Somewhere all of us who are the church, have a place in that expression. In a busy marketplace with all the sights and sounds of the fast-paced twentieth century, the church can be there as a faithful witness, communicating.

Telling the Story
of the Local Church

The People... and the Plan

What would be a good communications program for your church and how can you go about developing it?

How far should you go? What is in good taste and what should be avoided? How do you determine how to make the best use, from the church's standpoint, of limited resources? When should you seek to utilize "free" representation and when should you consider "paid" space or time?

The word "planning" is vital to a sound communications program for the church, and it is equally vital for the people, with whom it begins.

In a typical experience, a layperson is named to head a committee to improve communications within the church. He calls a meeting of the people he knows who may have some interest or talents in this general field.

"Our job is to check out communications and make sure they are set for the year," he begins. "Now we have the weekly bulletin, the minister will see to that." He checks this item from a listing on a flip sheet and proceeds to number two.

"We do need a telephone committee." A general murmur of assent from the group. "Let's see, Jane. I wonder if you could continue with that; you did such a fine job last year?"

"Sue said she would be chairman," Jane reports, "I took the liberty of asking her." A little laughter greets this statement and some restlessness sets in as she continues to speak.

"I plan to take one section of the membership but we will need some other people. Any volunteers?"

A woman responds affirmatively and other names are proposed. The flip sheet takes on more names and the chairman proceeds with the next item on the listing.

"John has something about the Brotherhood event," he says. John talks about the event and says that they plan to put up posters and send out mailers.

"Well, that's about it," the chairperson concludes. "We will meet again before annual meeting. Maybe we can get some other people in on this?"

How could the people involved in this session have been strengthened and encouraged in what well may be called a ministry of communication, involving both utilization of technical skills and talents and a commitment to the Lord and His Body, the Church?

THE PEOPLE

Communications within the Body of Christ may aptly be considered as a network to keep the various parts of the body supplied with needed contact one to another. Although the pastor communicates something of the life of the church wherever he or she goes, the pastor is not "communications." Neither can a governing board or a particular organization within the church take on this overall communications ministry.

To be a continuously functioning network, communications must have a place in the structure of the individual church bringing together people for this purpose from many aspects of church life. A structured communications network acting in responsibility to the governing board or to the pastor would facilitate the dissemination of information both internally and externally. Although mass communication can never replace the personal invitation, it is a modern form of evangelism that extends that invitation.

The clergy should be a part—but not necessarily the center—of the church's communication process.

When communications represents a network of people, what evolves is an overview of church life, far broader, far more encompassing than any one person's circle of concern. It would provide:

1. time for each person to contribute about every area of church life; and

2. exploration of available means of communicating this life.

Members of the network would have definite terms, and regular provision would be made for new membership. The minister might want to attend the meetings or might serve as a resource person. If the group functions effectively, the minister will not be the major "producer," nor should the minister be placed in this role through interest and support.

The communications director does not necessarily need journalism training or experience. Nor does that person need to be a skillful writer. As a coordinator, he would need to be well acquainted with the church and the membership, and have a high degree of commitment.

Many churches now have one person assigned as a church communicator, which is a step toward having a unified communications program. This can be a help for the media that need an instant resource person, but it is a help that could be multiplied many times over through having more people involved and knowledgeable. A network coordinated by a communications director would also minimize needless duplication as unity developed and grew. The director would keep in close touch with the people serving in the network. One of these members, or the director, would serve as liaison to the governing body of the church. Some member of the committee might be named special consultant to the minister to provide special communications help when needed. Most ministers called upon to make a statement to the press on matters of public interest would welcome assistance in drafting such a statement. Other members would serve as liaison to the youth, to the women's organizations (or, conversely, these groups and organizations might appoint a representative to be in the communications network).

With communicators present in every area of church life, the listing of responsibilities would include:

The Governing Board
The Ministers

Men's Organization
Evangelism
Missionary and Outreach
Property and Grounds
Building Program
Financial
Christian Education
Church School
Women's Organizations
Youth Organizations

While the committee may be spending most of its time tackling specific communications problems, preparing for coverage of events and programs, it should have enough flexibility to put itself "in workshop" when the occasion demands that it take on special aspects of the communications task. For example, it might want to consider updating public information materials through which the church represents itself to new and prospective members. It might want to inaugurate a church-wide communications project

Saturday's church section in a metropolitan daily is highly competitive.

such as a film, an information newsletter, or an interrelated project with another church.

Perhaps the Church School leadership has long wanted more time and ways to share what is happening in this area with others. Perhaps the youngsters are coming to grips with the Gospel and finding new approaches in their lives. (Have you ever read a fifth-graders' version of one of the parables?) Perhaps there is a special program coming up and the overworked staff would really like more people to know about it. But where do they begin? Even to contact the people poses a problem.

Sometimes a person alert to the need of telling others, and aware of how to do it, takes on communications for the particular church group of which he or she is a part. Valuable at the moment, his efforts may in time present a distorted picture of the church. ("I see where the Brotherhood is having another banquet. Is eating the only thing your church does?" For John Smith, who regularly contacts the papers about Brotherhood events, such a remark would be a puzzle. He was publicizing the church. Wasn't that what he should be doing?)

A communications network would lend support to every area of church life through utilizing people where they are and by encouraging specialization whereby talents could be developed, broadened, and extended. The communications group could have further access to all the special talents within the church through establishing what we call a Talent Bank.

The Talent Bank
(With Cross-referencing)

```
Blake, Jane E.
Address
Phone
Photography, 35mm, Color, BW, Processes
B/W only; Music: plays guitar, composes.
```

```
Bowden, James A.
Address
Phone
Film. Has done super-8, editing, scripting. Has
no camera.
```

```
Bond, Alfred:
Address
Phone
Former advertising agency copy chief; will not
do publicity but will advise; Photography, has
35mm camera, color only. No processing. Likes
to teach.
```

Photography: Color

Blake, Jane E., Address, Phone. Has 35mm camera, no processing.

Bond, Alfred, Address, Phone. Has 35mm camera; no processing.

Estill, Mary, Address, Phone. Has 35mm camera; no processing. Has slide projector/screen.

Film:

Bowden, James A., Address, Phone. Editing, scripting, shooting. No camera.

Writing:

George, James, Address, Phone. Former newspaper editor. Brochures, news stories, features.

Gregg, Harry, Address, Phone. Writes for own enjoyment but would like to help out. Willing to gather facts and be edited.

Foster, Margaret, Address, Phone. Free-lance writer. Would like to teach. Will help on bulletin, but no publicity.

Other card categories:
Music
Teaching
Publicity
TV/Radio
Drama
Audio Cassette
Planning
Reviewing Communication
Annual Report
Fact-gathering/Interviewing
Liaison with Media

List names and particulars on separate cards in each category. Cards can be removed or new ones added as situation dictates. Talent Bank Cards should be periodically reviewed and processed by members of the communications committee to be sure everyone who wants to offer talents has an opportunity to do so.

Equipment Bank:

Cameras:
  Blake, Jane E.: Yashica 35mm SLR
  Bond, Alfred: Canon 35mm SLR
  Estill, Mary: Canon 35mm SLR

Slide Projectors/Screen:
  Estill, Mary: Automatic projector, carousel/
    screen. Will loan for use by competent person
    for church program; or will operate herself.

Movie Cameras
Movie Projectors
Movie Editors/Splicers
Cassette Recorders
Extra Speakers
Videotape Equipment
Photocopy Equipment
Electric or Good Manual Typewriter

Notation should state under what circumstances equipment will be loaned or whether person owning it will operate it for the church.

Now people in the network can specialize in the media or area for which they are best suited.

John Smith, who formerly mailed out letters about the Brotherhood, contacted the newspapers about the Brotherhood, and put up notices on the bulletin board, could now attend a communications meeting knowing that there will be people to help him tell others. Perhaps he has already established a good relationship with the editor of the local newspaper. As a network member, he could develop that particular relationship and could impart information about other aspects of his church to the editor.

Through his church communications meetings, John would be informed about plans and directions within the church. And he would be able to supply his editor friend (and other newspaper editors) with the information they needed when they needed it. He would know their own particular requirements; and he would understand about deadlines. He would make sending announcements—and suggestions for other stories—a regular part of his joyous service. In time, he would be rewarded with a call:

"Look, John, this is Raymond Brown of *The News*. You sent us that note about the migrant family your church 'adopted.' We'd like to get some pictures and talk to these people. Could you arrange it?"

Later, some people would call the long feature on the adopted migrant family "good publicity" for the church. But members of the communications network with new understandings would talk about how and what their church communicated through this article

and what other possibilities they might have for such communication.

While John continued in his approach to editors and reporters, another team member would be exploring the routes of communication available through direct mailings. At the last meeting, John said the Brotherhood was still having a prayer breakfast each Thursday morning and it was open to all men of the community. Ann, who was in charge of direct mail, collected the facts about it and composed a couple of letters. One went to each man of the local congregation, extending to him a personal invitation to the breakfasts and suggesting that he might want to ask others to attend with him. The other letter went to the pastors of the neighboring churches including them and the men of their churches in the invitation to fellowship together.

A young person might be intrigued with the ways that bulletin boards and posters could be utilized. When it was time to place the posters in stores, youngsters who are so often cut off from any service to their church would be willing hands.

THE PLAN

After the people comes the plan. What are some of the obvious needs during the year, the events which will make a big demand on available resources and provide a challenge to creative communication? The communications group will find its most useful tool is the common calendar.

The Calendar

All members of the network should have a calendar large enough to record events of importance and daily notations. All the deadlines incidental to communicating an event can be clearly listed. Everyone has a calendar, and no one is left in doubt about a date. These dates also need to be verified and confirmed with the calendar listings of the church office. It's important that all times, dates, and places announced for an event agree.

Major events are usually known twelve months in advance: seasonal observances, preaching missions, homecomings, anniversaries, vacation church school, special seminars, courses, musical events, missionary programs, participation in community projects.

At the beginning of the year, the calendar is reviewed. Which events need outside coverage? What kind? Weekly newspaper in the area, religious news section of a big daily, smaller dailies? Radio and TV?

Contact with other churches? Direct mail? Posters? Signs or billboards?

The Church Calendar: the Communications Year

Events listed are generalized. Different denominations will, of course, have different types of activities worthy of external communication. The authors hope those listed here will be a stimulus to the preparation of a similar list for your particular church.

JANUARY

Annual church meeting.
Epiphany season service.
Feast of Lights/Burning of Greens.
Election of vestry, elders, deacons.
Review of past year, projections for future.
Adoption of budget.
Tree planting (or later in some climates).
World Day of Prayer.

FEBRUARY

Plans for Lenten observances.
Special speakers scheduled to visit the church.
Ecumenical activities.
Church School programs.

MARCH

Symbolistic activities of Lent: stripping of altar, imposition of ashes.
A prayer for Good Friday.
Any retreat or other prayer-related activity.
Making of palm crosses for Palm Sunday.
Good time for a weekly newspaper article or radio comment on the significance of Lent in modern life.
Review a Lenten book.

APRIL

Decoration of church for Easter.
Familiarization with Easter traditions of other countries and other religions.
The Paschal meal.
The Paschal candle.
Baptism, confirmation, and other events taking place at this time.
Any special visitors.
Record Easter attendance.
Participation in ecumenical services.
Special music.

MAY

May fete.
Story on church school or day school.
Spring programs and graduations.
Church picnic or homecoming.
Mother's Day: a special tribute (Salute the Christian Mother of the Year in your town.)
Refurbishing of church grounds: landscaping, "spring cleaning."

JUNE

Vacation Church School plans.
Parish summer camp or church's youth going to a church camp.
Vacation plans: how to support the church while you're gone.
If minister is leaving town, who will substitute for him while he is away.
Any summer recreational program for the community in which church participates.
Father's Day.
Story on St. John the Baptist.

JULY

How the church celebrates Independence Day.
Pentecost—what it means.
Photos of church picnic or other activity.
An all-church trip.
A letter from a church member who has gone to some interesting place such as Russia, the Holy Land, etc.
A youth work party in another country (Mexico, for example).
Overseas work—a story on how much the church spends outside itself.

AUGUST

Resumption of Church School plans.
A story on what a church secretary does.
A personal feature on some outstanding church member or someone who has worked on a community project.
Athletic events the church has sponsored or will sponsor (swim team, riding team, basketball, football, etc.).
What a church has to do to get ready for fall.

SEPTEMBER

Church School opens.
Fall programs announced by church groups—youth, women, men, etc.
New Bible classes begin.
Plans for fall bazaar or carnival.

Visiting ministers or other guests.

College students are going back to school (story on church attendance of college students).

Blessing of the pets.

A special Church School opening program.

Participation in fall community events.

OCTOBER

Bazaar (pictures).

Financial drive (if there is an annual one, it may be around this time).

All Saints Day service.

Good time to announce building program, any expanded services, new minister, new staff help, etc.

Good time to pay tribute to someone who deserves special recognition.

NOVEMBER

Feed-the-hungry baskets.

Plans to help the elderly (the forgotten ones) between now and Christmas.

Home services for sick and shut-ins.

Advent and its events.

Special prayer services.

Ecumenical events.

DECEMBER

Preholiday activities.

A sermon on the season.

Special Christmas services.

Nativity scene or choral festival or other event.

Return of some former members for Christmas.

What about midnight service—how it got started, background on it.

Decoration of church.

After Christmas: What happens to all those poinsettias?

Hospital visiting during Christmas.

Holiday Church School programs.

And throughout the year whenever appropriate:

Dedications.

Groundbreakings.

Consecrations.

Conferences (where church is host).

Activities of members: election to high office, awards or honors, publication of book, art show, invention, etc.

Distinguished visitors.

Establishment of new church program (or expansion of one now offered).

Church stimulating interest in arts (with its own art show or a religious subject section in a community art show).

Publication of a church history.

Program for evangelism (such as recognition of visitors, revival, etc.).

Development of community program: drug abuse, teen runaways, counseling, activities for singles.

Series on church observances, symbolism.

Comments from church member who has visited interesting place and observed religious customs there.

A series or single article on area of current interest—ecology, ethics in business, dignity of dying, teen marriages, abortion, etc.

Need for church schools.

Story on whether or not churches should be taxed.

How do you go about "hiring" a new minister?

Christian aspect of swearing-in ceremony for mayor, council, judges, etc.

The role of the church in sports, including competitive athletics.

The calendar may offer other opportunities to communicate the church in terms of ministry to the elderly, to the community as a whole, to youth. In these categories come crime prevention programs, counseling efforts, overseas work, support of community art, drama, other forms of culture.

This kind of participation may suggest a thoughtful article on the role of the church in culture. Who can write it? If your talent bank has been carefully prepared and cross-filed, you might find the names of one or more persons who can write and who are also involved in drama, music, or the arts. This linkage of expertise is one of the most useful products of the talent and equipment bank. It eliminates guesswork, time-consuming trial and error. You can put your finger on one or more prospects just right for the job in the shortest possible time.

A serious study of the year-long work in which the church is involved will suggest a number of opportunities for thoughtful articles and possible ways to illustrate them. Bringing these together with the people who can best prepare them is a legitimate function of the communications committee. Such material will generally be received with enthusiasm by the local media, particularly if the offering is prepared to satisfy both their specific subject and their mechanical requirements. It is always a good idea to firm up all such possibilities in advance by discussing them with the appropriate news person. He or she may offer guidelines to follow in developing the idea, and will answer questions such as how long should it be? What angle? Interview format or straight feature? What kinds of pictures? What deadline?

A well-kept scrapbook gives access to the history of the church.

Communications by Chart Pad

Write on a chart pad the following data concerning the event to be communicated:

Date.
Time.
Place.
Event and title or subject.
Speaker's name and title.
Subject of the talk.
Purpose of gathering (commemorative, fund-raising, educational, etc.).
Cost of attending and where to get tickets.
Use of money.
Number of people expected.
Key committees and their members.
Any related events or activities (meals, seminars, discussion groups, receptions).
Some brief facts about the host church: size, when founded, name of minister, any key ongoing church program that ties into the event.

Fill in the blanks. Do it early enough so that you are aware of what facts are not in hand and can plan to acquire them. After each topic, note the requisite information or where it can be obtained and who will be assigned to track it down.

Keep the pad posted in a prominent place. Set another meeting by which time all data should be in and all blanks filled. Have someone transfer the data on the pad to 8½" by 11" paper, typed, double-spaced, with the name and phone number of a contact person at the top. It is suggested that a single resource or contact person serve each medium for at least one year. In that way, the news editor of that medium will come to know and trust the contact and will feel freer to print what he or she submits.

Usually this method of writing will not have to be resorted to for long. It will be noted how simple the process is. Some reluctant writers will come forward, obviously more relaxed about offering their talents. This kind of approach is useful in communicating major events where the approach is a straightforward rendition of facts. Other kinds of communication tasks may require more personal approaches, but the committee can still function in terms of planning, offering input and research, reviewing every aspect of the communication task and putting it into perspective.

Communications may be aimed at three major targets: events, programs, and people. We have fit events and programs into our communications year; now let us take a look at people as subject matter for communicating the church.

There is a story in every person in the church. Your own congregation can provide material for personal vignettes, self help, specific experience, or other types of articles of broad interest. You may have to dig for these but, like a search for any treasure, it can be exciting and immensely satisfying. Ordinary people doing out-of-the ordinary things, deeply Christian things. This is grist for the communications process of the church; it is also food for thought within the communications group who must deal themselves with existence, significance, and responsibilities. As presenters of information, do they also see themselves as agents of change? What it is we really want to say and how we can best say it in the wraparound of the daily events of our lives is a discipline of communications basic to us all.

The person, who invents, who gardens, who builds furniture, who does wood carving is a member of the church. His Christianity may be enunciated as he explains his work or his purpose in pursuing it. He may need some help in expressing himself—a good listener who provides a word or a phrase to clarify his thinking, his direction. Relayed to paper, it is his story with depth, dimension, and power. There are many such stories whose overt or underlying Christian themes may be portrayed as commitment, stewardship, mission, brotherhood. It is the raw thread that reveals itself in the interview, and becomes a part of the fabric which is the story.

We recognize the duty of every Christian to be an evangelist, to tell others of the Good News. Some can, gladly and articulately. Some cannot. "I just can't express myself in words. I can't look directly at someone and talk about my faith—yet there must be some way." And of course there is. The medium for communicating the faith today is not only verbal, it is written and it is visual. We have a responsibility to tell, to use the mechanical features of our age to the glory of God. It is not to seek numbers, to fill sanctuaries, to establish an image, to build a reputation. It is to share the gift that we know in Christ Jesus.

CHAPTER TWO

The Church Meets Itself in the Church Bulletin

When the Apostle Paul wrote his letters to the church at Corinth and Ephesus, he used a simple medium, the letter; and he conveyed a personal message that spans the centuries and provides a springboard for both personal and corporate renewal even today.

Certainly no church publication can replace, add to, or take away from God's Word as contained in the Scriptures. Yet every church publication should look to be an instrument to convey that power in Christ in its own particular way. For the church bulletin to be that kind of publication requires neither extraordinary amounts of money nor extraordinary talents. It does require at least one person or more, either clergy or lay, with dedication and commitment.

In America today, some quarter of a million congregations have the opportunity through weekly or semi-monthly publications to share the Good News with others through newsletters and bulletins mailed into more than 137 million homes. But has that dynamic and lively Gospel somehow gotten lost or obscured in a mass of verbiage and distracting appearance? Or is there more to it than that?

Because of the secularism and materialism of our age, some say, people are indifferent to religion. Others say that indifference comes from the parade of trivialities which the typical church program offers to the public. Conflict and dissension has alienated some people; others are alienated because the church presents an unreal harmony which eliminates or ignores the dissident.

But whether indifference to the church or conflict within the church, it is no less likely that these same forces were also present when Paul wrote:

> "But we beseech you, brethren, to respect those who labor among you and are over you in the Lord and admonish you, and to esteem them very highly in love because of their work. Be at peace among yourselves. And we exhort you, brethren, admonish the idlers, encourage the fainthearted, help the weak, be patient with them all. See that none of you repays evil for evil, but always seek to do good to one another and to all. Rejoice always, pray constantly, give thanks in all circumstances; for this is the will of God in Christ Jesus for you." 1 Thessalonians 5:12–18

Stand aside from your involvement in your own church publication; the pressures of deadlines, the problems of being up-to-date, the needs of the congregation, and look at your publication in what may be a new way.

Into whatever hands the church paper falls, it is *at that moment* the church to them. They may choose to toss it aside; but if they read it, the publication at that instant takes its place alongside the Sunday morning service, a meeting of the congregation, a call from the visitation committee as the Body of Christ ministering to them. The publication as a ministering arm of the church presents a new criterion for editing with standards as basic as the Gospel itself.

> Does this publication bring life to the reader?
> Does it bring reconciliation and healing?
> Does it edify, build up, inform?

Far from being unobtainable goals, these are the questions that, placed in perspective, keep us confronted with the real issues, and that keep us open to diversity and change.

Does your publication minister to life? Or is it an illegible, flimsy sheet of paper that says, "We don't care?" The hard-to-read, grey looking publication makes an added statement: "We don't care enough about *you* to make this legible." More weight to the paper, more contrast between the printed word and the page not only presents an easier-to-read publication, it suggests strength, stability, and *life.* Isn't that available in generous supply in your church?

Economics dictates the choice of production method employed by most churches. Budgets rarely have adequate means for all expenses. With reproduction costs ranging from a few dollars to hundreds of dollars, the final choice is a question of budget priorities. Yet one point cannot be overemphasized; a regularly issued church publication is no longer an optional expense. It is one of the most effective means of outreach possible to a congregation. In some instances, it may be an individual's only contact with the church.

If you are entering the publications field for the first time, you need to know how much it will cost. Or if you have been publishing for some time, perhaps it's time to recheck how your publication dollar is being spent. Although costs will vary from place to place, the factors influencing those costs remain constant. We have prepared a listing of those factors as a series of questions in a publication profile.

Are you really getting the best publication possible with the money you have to spend? You will be better prepared to answer that after you fill in the details on your publication profile.

PUBLICATION PROFILE

How Many Copies Will Be Printed?

Bulk mailing rates begin at 200 copies, and if you have not obtained a bulk mailing permit for a nonprofit organization, a visit to your local post office will be the first order of business. After obtaining your permit (there's a fee), you will pay a rate based on weight. By the way, each mailing must be identical in size (no partial stuffing) to qualify as bulk mail. Check other postal regulations.

Mailing, then, is a factor in determining how many copies will be printed. To cut the number of copies printed and mailed by 20, 25, or usually anything under 100, makes little reduction, if any at all, in costs. The most frequent complaint we hear about church

Publish Glad Tidings: Church newsletters come in many shapes and sizes.

mailings are from people who for one reason or another were removed from the mailing list. Such removal is invariably viewed as an affront by people whose membership may be elsewhere but whose concern is still intertwined in some way with the life of your church. When mailing lists are checked, and they should be reviewed periodically, it's wise to have several people, with knowledge about the church and its membership, past, and present, on the job.

In addition to correct names and addresses of members, the publication mailing list should include these kinds of names:

People who live nearby who have visited the church, or any visitors who have some ongoing connection with the church.

The leadership or clergy of neighboring churches, particularly of other denominations, with whom your church might have contacts, and others with an ecumenical interest.

Other denominational publications which might use your publication to keep abreast of news about your church.

Should you mail your publication to the local press? Before making an instant reply in the affirmative, answer this question. Can you mail your publication to the local press without reservations about the follow-up on its content? A publication mailed to the news media approaches the category of the news release or information in the public domain. Although professional ethics might seem to dictate that you or the church would be consulted before the news used information from your publication, it is not bound—except by its own sense of professionalism, propriety, and competence in writing—to verify its information. This is not to say that church publications should not be mailed to the local newspapers and media. It is *most* appropriate that they do receive your publication, but be aware of possible problems. It is a part of the challenge of editing a church publication that its content be helpful also to the news media.

How Is Your Publication Printed?

Mimeograph more than 10 years old?
Mimeograph less than 10 years old?
Duplicator with or without scanner?
Offset or multilith?

The advance of technology, a frequent phrase in theological discussions, makes a much slower entrance into the rooms that house the church's office equipment. And a corollary to the equipment problem is the people problem. The most sophisticated equipment remains useless without a person who will learn its operation. So, choice of printing methods depends on availability both of equipment and personnel. If the church equipment is antiquated and there is little or no permanent office help, a secretarial service with an up-to-date duplicating machine can produce your church publication at a cost that's probably well within the budget.

Offset or multilith in a print shop costs considerably more but permits use of photographs and offers all the quality of fine printing. A medium-to-large size church which sends out a variety of printed materials should consider investing in duplicating and offset equipment which would handle all its mailings, as well as cards, posters, letterheads for stationery. Another option, and one used extensively in industry, is the cooperative arrangement. Buy in, or buy time, with another church or two. Each has its own "day", but to avoid confusion make sure all arrangements are in writing. If yours is a small church, there may be a large church in your area with equipment that they would gladly "lease" for a day. Or if you are a large church, this may be a means of improving the equipment you have. Cooperation in such matters can lay the groundwork for strengthened relationships for all the churches.

If you're spending $50 or more a month on reproduction processes (excluding the cost of paper) and you have an office staff or someone who would operate the equipment, it's time to consider purchasing a duplicator. (Current models range in price form $800 to $1,800.) The country's leading manufacturers, Gestetner and A. B. Dick, have distributors in every major city (check the yellow pages) and all companies will provide information on application, cost, and service on the machines they sell.

If your church has a mimeograph or duplicating machine, have it serviced regularly. If your copy is coming out smudged or unclear, the machine may not be inking properly. However, there are two other major reasons for fuzzy reproduction: improper cutting of the stencil and inferior paper.

What Kind of Paper Do You Use?

If the words (and art) in your bulletin or leaflet stand clearly and sharply defined, with no hovering shadows or imperceptible shapes, then reproduction method and paper have married well and produced a good-looking (and readable) offspring. But most often this union fares badly, not because of printing method but because of the paper. All paper costs, but the difference between what you are currently using and another more appropriate grade may amount to a saving of $2 per issue. And if that kind of saving is critical to your church, there's still another way of obtaining the best paper for your process at an unmatched price. Be a good shopper. Paper companies frequently sell off odd lots to make way for new supplies. After you know the weight and type of paper, check with these companies.

A talk with the paper people in your town could be the biggest single step you could make toward having a readable publication. Here are some of the comments we've gathered from them:

"Many people use a slick #20 mimeograph paper when they need a #24 vellum."

"If the paper is too thin, the ink bleeds through."

"If the paper has no texture, then it cannot absorb the ink, which slides across the page."

"If the paper is too heavy, the ink smears."

"Paper is our business. We would be glad to show what we have and tell how it can be used."

Another word of caution about paper. Nowadays it comes in an array of attractive colors. It's tempting to try the unusual (along with some new shade of ink), but readability still remains as the final criterion in making this decision. We've seen publications in greens and blues and yellows. With black ink, they have been readable. With colored ink, they have not.

Who Does the Labor?

There may be single-handed publications, but most church leaflets require a minimum staff of two or three people. The editor prepares the copy and a general (or final) layout. Another person types or cuts the stencil and runs the machine. Still another runs the addressograph and handles the mailing. In some churches, lay people give their services for these tasks; others have paid staff to include these duties or some part of them. Part of these services are "farmed out" to print shops. If you currently have a salaried employee operating the mimeograph machine and folding and mailing, investigate what a small print shop or secretarial firm would charge for one of the newer duplicating processes. If "getting out the bulletin" is a regular office crisis, then it's time to consider some alternatives that would free the church staff for other calls they have on their time and talents. But getting the facts on your church publication means knowing how many people are regularly involved with its issuance and the contribution that each makes week after week to getting it in the mails.

How Often Do You Publish?

When the bulletin also serves as the Sunday morning service sheet (listing hymns and order of service),

weekly publication is mandatory. The Sunday worshiper as a captive reader may be an advantage to circulation, and there can be some financial saving in this dual system, but we believe each loses in this process.

The service sheet reproduced on art paper that reinforces the liturgy of the season can be a dramatic message to the person in the pew that its condensed counterpart in the bulletin can never quite achieve. The sheet also provides space for any other information that might be helpful on Sunday morning. Some of this information may conceivably be duplicated in the bulletin, but most of it would not. The bulletin that does not contain the Sunday service sheet can be directed totally to the reader away from the church. The mailed publication could have a design and format particularly aimed to attract readers at home, and with more space for reflective articles and fewer repetitious areas of "scheduling."

The publication not tied to a service sheet may be printed on alternating weeks, particularly if the church is small, allowing for maximum use of money and time.

Some churches have gone "magazine" style with monthly publications that contain a pull-out calendar. And even more are using a combination monthly publication along with a weekly bulletin. The monthly magazine (sometimes nothing more elaborate than mimeograph sheets stapled together book style) permits within a single issue more comprehensive coverage of the life of the church. The obvious drawback would be the time gap between preparation of copy and forthcoming events. This is the gap that larger churches span with a single page weekly.

A more extensive monthly publication could be the next step in communication at your church with one or two committed people providing the forward motion.

How Much Does Your Publication Cost?

With the Publication Profile Chart as a guide, determine how much your publication or publications cost. You will want to include the cost of mailing, printing, paper, ink, and supplies. For the cost of staff, prorate the hours spend on publications. If calculations are on a yearly basis, divide by the number of issues to find your per-copy cost. More than an interesting exercise, the results will provide you with ammunition for decision making. You may also discover that a much more attractive publication can be obtained with little or no increase in cost. Know what you are paying—now.

Publication Profile Chart

How Many Copies Will Be Printed?
Mailed?

200	300	400	500	600	700	800	900	1000	1200	1500	2000

How Often Published?

Weekly   Semimonthly   Monthly   Monthly plus Weekly

What Process?

Mimeograph   Duplicator   Offset   Multilith

Where

Church office   Secretarial service   Print shop

Paper Used Per Issue

Type of paper (weight, color, texture)   Reams (500 sheets per ream)

Other Supplies Needed

Ink   Stencils   Stencil art masters   Offset art

Paid Staff

Prorated hours of: Secretary   Clergy   Other help

Cost

Per issue   Annually

After the Profile

Once you start talking to people about your publications, you will begin to get a picture that seems engraved in stone. Fortunately, it is not.

Take Mr. McFoy, for instance. For the past ten years he has printed the bulletin. With rising costs, he absorbs the extra for the church. Although he's not too happy about that, he's reluctant to assert himself. Or it may be that Mr. McFoy, with obsolete equipment and inadequate help, charges the church more than the prevailing price for such work. Yes, Mr. McFoy has printed the publication for years. Doesn't it seem time that someone talked with *him* personally? Then there's the elusive Helen. She would like to run the machine again. She stopped temporarily because of a family crisis and was never contacted again about it.

The priest or minister who becomes involved with publications finds ample opportunity for pastoring within this ministry. Yet the same opportunity exists for the lay person who has accepted the responsibility for church publications.

In more and more churches lay people have plugged in to this aspect of church life and assumed responsibility for areas once considered exclusively the priest's or minister's domain. The priesthood of the laity, far from being a threatening development, helps carry the load more effectively. Nowhere is this more true than in the field of publications.

"We underrate our lay people in tragic ways," a director of a religious training program recently commented. "Ministers and lay persons often are put into a superior-inferior relationship. But lay people have demonstrated their ability to function as effectively as what we have come to expect from trained ministers." (The Rev. Ron Sunderland, director of continuing education, the Institute of Religion, Texas Medical Center, Houston.)

THE CHURCH MEETS ITSELF IN THE CHURCH BULLETIN

For most ministers and priests, production of the weekly publication without adequate assistance consumes valuable time in large bites.

"What a headache!" We've heard that more than once! And publications equally suffer. Without leadership sensitive to the potential of the printed word and skilled in putting it together in attractive form, the publication may seem more a weekly harbinger of bad news than good.

Within every congregation stand one or two people —sometimes unknown, frequently untapped—with all the skills and talents needed to enter into this ministry. Let us dispense with the stereotype that says that is the clergy's responsibility. Editing is a ministry just as often for the unordained as the ordained.

CHAPTER THREE

The Parish Newsletter: Now That You Are Editor

"Let the words of my mouth and the meditation of my heart be acceptable in thy sight, O Lord. . . ."

The psalmist's prayer could well be offered daily by anyone who is in charge of a church publication. The prayer directs us to look not only at the words we use but also at where our thinking is centered. It calls us to see beyond that which is most visible.

And so it is with editing. How often do we pause to hear what is really being said? Arbitrary judgments, put-downs, negative approaches, can be instruments of death as well as of love, faith, hope, and trust. That a statement is taken from the Scriptures makes it no less a weapon if a writer so chooses. As communicators, we must be vigilant; as editors, we must be willing to accept our responsibility for that task.

In a local church, the pastor as shepherd of the flock surely stands as the guiding authority for any publication, but when "press time" arrives, it is usually someone else who has compiled the material and placed it in the form in which it is printed. That person is for all practical purposes the editor. We believe that church publications benefit from having duties and responsibilities clearly defined.

The clergy may provide much of the content but that person who is editor commits himself to:

1. Gathering news, information, and articles to provide an ongoing and up-to-date picture of life in the church.
2. Editing and soliciting articles contributed by others.
3. Writing stories.
4. Determining format.
5. Preparing the layout.
6. Finalizing for printing.

A minister may carry out these functions or the duties may be shared with a layperson or church secretary. Editing is certainly best accomplished with the minister's active support and encouragement. A minister who seeks to have a lively publication which serves the community of his church and beyond might consider these questions:

- Do I regularly share information about church or community which would be useful in the publication?
- Do I provide background information to the editor that would be helpful?
- Do I speak directly to the congregation through the publication on vital matters?
- Do I take time to pass along suggestions and comments to the editor?
- Do I permit the editor to exercise his duties or do I in some way decree "no editing" to submitted material?

Editing, like surgery, is approached with caution. Yet everyone benefits from careful and selected editing, not least of all the writer who may be conveying a great deal more than he or she intends. When "death" creeps into writing, it is the editor's task to strike it out. What do we mean by death? Read the following paragraphs and take note.

"With property values increasing steadily, the church board agreed this week to go ahead with the purchase of the adjoining lots at a cost of $45,000. We could have obtained it for much less in times past if action had been taken on financing.

"Since money for the purchase is not in the budget, a special drive for funds is now necessary. Everyone should be able to contribute. You will be contacted either by letter or personally to inform you about the purchase. We hope to conclude the drive before summer when most people will be using their resources for vacation."

Did you spot the culprits?

We could have obtained it for much less in times past . . .
Why didn't you?

If action had been taken. . . .
I always knew we had a bunch of do-nothings on the board.

Since money for the purchase is not in the budget . . .
You mean the board is buying something without money and they expect us to pay for it!

Everyone should be able to contribute. . . .
I don't see how we can afford to give now.

When most people will be using their resources for vacation. . . .
What resources? What vacation? Maybe this church is too rich for us.

How would you have written this story to express the faith the decision represents, to reflect the board's commitment, to challenge the congregation's support? As an editor, what would you do if such a story was submitted to you by the head of the board? Use the story as presented? (Remember, the author is the top lay official of the church.) Would you have deleted some of the offending phrases? Or would you have contacted the writer and discussed the story further? Our choice would be to contact the author, the board official. We would encourage the writer to tell us about the board's plans, the history of the decision, what is needed from the congregation.

Many church people approach writing for the church publication with reluctance, while those in offices of leadership in particular welcome the opportunity to talk out what they have to convey. The result may be an article prepared by the official or it may be written by the editor from the official's information.

Effective communication requires knowing the source of information. The editorial "we" and the "we" who are the church are alike in representing a body of people. Who then speaks for that body? With the spoken word, we can see who speaks. With the written word, we cannot.

The unity of the church is established in Christ; it does not preclude individuality. The effective church publication which reveals "many members incorporate" catches the sound of many voices.

TO CAPTURE THE SOUND OF MANY VOICES

What are some of the ways a church publication can present many and varied expressions of faith, even with limited space?

The Quote

Probably the most popular method, because of its simplicity, is the "borrowed" column. Although quoting from other publications is a legitimate means of obtaining various viewpoints, if not also the sanction of the wisdom of the ages, beware of two pitfalls in quote selection. Filler simply to occupy space is an obvious device and not one designed to encourage readership. If you consistently use material with little direct relationship to the ongoing life of the church, take note. The second caution concerns copyright laws. You must have permission to use material from copyrighted publications except for reviews or limited references which name the publication.

In any publication, a ready supply of copy or art is essential for make-up. Rather than being a haphazard selection of something hopefully inspiring or entertaining, this material by careful planning can be integral to the thrust of communications.

Seek and you shall find, but be prepared to edit— even a bishop. Take that 300-word speech of his given at a conference on evangelism and printed in your denomination's regional publication. In your church publication it becomes:

> "Let no man thirst when water is available and we have that water in Jesus Christ. Evangelism is here; evangelism is now."

Another church is sponsoring the event, but youth of all churches are invited to participate.

> "When a winner makes a mistake, he says, 'I was wrong.' When a loser makes a mistake, he says, 'It wasn't my fault.' "
> Winners and losers will be under study at the teen workshop on self-esteem to be held at St. Peter's Church next month. Teens from this congregation who would like to attend are invited to register now.

The date is June 24. The liturgical calendar of the church says it is the Nativity of St. John the Baptist. A

Bible synopsis lists John as the only child of Elizabeth and Zechariah and gives some comments. Without being a historian, it's possible to observe the day.

> "After me comes he who is mightier than I, the thong of whose sandals I am not worthy to stoop down and untie. I have baptized you with water; but he will baptize you with the Holy Spirit" (Mark 1:7–8).
> St. John the Baptist, whose birthday is June 24, is sometimes called the "last and greatest of the prophets." The forerunner of his cousin, Jesus, he was the only. . . .

The mailman delivers a treasury of information in brochures, newsletters, magazines. Draw from that wealth and invest it in new ways.

Fact #1—from a national report on mission:
"There are fifty towns with a total population of 500,000 in the Miura Peninsula of Japan, and now open on the peninsula is a training center established by a grant from the national missionary fund."

Fact #2—from the local church:
Your gift to the missionary fund is used far and near. This month it helped establish a training center in Japan.

Fact #3—A special envelope is available in the church for missionary offerings.

Your story:
Did you know that your missionary dollar is at work now in Japan? On the Miura Peninsula, the lay training center opened this month through a $10,000 grant of the National Missionary Fund. Gifts for the missionary fund may be made at any time and special envelopes in the hymn rack in the sanctuary are provided for such gifts.

Specifically, in your quest for "planned filler" you should look for quotations of either a few sentences or brief paragraphs which:

- Enhance our knowledge of the church either as we know it individually or as a part of a larger unit or adjudicatory;
- Strengthen ecumenical ties;
- Voice Christian response to some of today's problems;
- Introduce us to other churchmen both living and dead, and to contemporary leadership;
- Inform us about our own Christian history, liturgical year, or worship.

Even with copyright laws, resources are boundless— from the Bible to a daily newspaper, from the biography of a statesman to a denominational magazine. It's a search in which many people may participate, and it is most fruitful when many people do share in this way in their own publication. But there are other means also in which the congregation may share in the ministry of the printed word in their church.

The Report

Many people will say if asked, "I abhor writing"; but the same people involved in some way in the life of the church will gladly write about that involvement. There is a double dividend in getting a personal report of a seminar, retreat, study group, in the report on the content of the study and in the reporter's reaction to it as well. Reviews of books and films provide a good springboard for personal commentaries made in a Christian context. Systematic leadership summaries with personal evaluation of aims and purposes are another means of incorporating personal viewpoints with factual content.

All contributions must be edited for consistency of style, for space, for clarity. Some rewriting may be necessary. Again, it is important that someone accept the task of editor whether it be church secretary, minister, or layperson. Let this not be the missing link in your publication chain. When every contribution is treated as inviolate, that not a word be touched, and a typist copies it line for line, communications suffer.

An editor will work with reporters and contributors to explain both publication requirements and the necessity of editing. On publication day in the church office, we might hear the following conversation:

"Hello, Mr. Jones, this is Ruth Brown in the church office. I'm editing the material for this week's bulletin and I want to thank you for your prompt article about the workshop. It's an interesting article and since it's so important for people to know about this event, I would like to use the story in two parts, repeating the time and place, of course. In this way, we would have information about the event in two issues with something new in each story and nothing would have to be cut because of space."

"Make whatever changes are needed? Thank you, I don't see anything else. It's a very good article and quite comprehensive. It should really help. . . ."

A reporter may be a member of the Bible class (what is the study this week?); the secretary of the organization; the participant in the seminar; the chairman of the committee; the originator of the activity; the reader of the book; someone with a "sermon" or witness or special expertise; the pastor or priest.

We believe readers appreciate knowing who contributed the articles so we recommend identification by headlines or bylines or signatures such as:

From the Pastor's Desk:

Project M Begins April 9

Decisions of Council

by Ann Moore

A Study of Galatians with Peggy

Another method of identification may come at the end of the story with use of the author's name at the conclusion. For meeting announcements and committee reports, routinely contributed by the same people, it's good to identify the source and it helps to personalize.

Jane Smith, president of the Sunshine class, asks all members to read *Mark*, Chapter Five, and bring their Bibles to class Sunday. If you have never attended this class, she invites you to visit and join in.

Such reports should be concise and succinct and indeed the church publication has little space for wordy dissertations. Yet much can be said in a few words by someone willing to serve as "eyes to see" and "ears to hear" for the congregation.

The Interview

Be alert to the talents and gifts in operation in your church. Ministries come in all sizes and shapes. We know a person who has been "the cook" at church for several decades, another who is "Mr. Fix-It" for anything broken, a couple who unfailingly call on anyone sick. These are not committee assignments or elected offices, but they are part of the "variety of gifts" at work in any church. The church publication which increases our awareness of this variety is in itself a gift.

There are times when an interview must necessarily set forth answers to questions either stated or implied, but for the most part that interview which seems more like a conversation between friends is the one that remains with us as a warm and personal visit. In such a setting and with a faith that describes us all as brothers, a relaxed openness is possible. Conversation moves freely to explore many areas. You may have some ideas about the destination but remember it is the subject who has the map. There are more suggestions about conducting an interview in chapter five, "Interviewing, A Service to the Media," which you will want to study. Extensive interviewing on a broad field of subject matter is hardly feasible for a weekly newsletter, but brief specialized interviews contribute greatly to a personalized publication.

When your desk seems stacked with masses of figures, notices of meetings, and details of scheduling, it may be time to dial a number and speak to:

• *The head of the finance committee.* How does this month's financial statement compare to similar periods last year? Is our level of stewardship up or down?

• *The minister of music.* I understand that you need singers to begin practice for the Easter cantata. Do they need to be "pros"? How do you feel about the part that music plays in the celebration of Easter?

• *The new president of the women's association.* What do you see as your role in the church today and does this differ from an earlier time in your life? What kind of direction do you envision for the organization this year?

• *A member involved with a community problem.* I understand that you are concerned about illiteracy and serve now on the board of the Literacy Council. How extensive is the problem of illiteracy? Is there some way members of this congregation might help?

• *A long-time church school teacher.* Do you find a difference now in the needs of children compared to your first years of teaching? What kind of questions do they ask? What grade do you teach?

• *A "prayer warrior."* Has prayer always been important in your life? Has God answered your prayers? Do you have a particularly vivid experience about a request you put to Him?

When it's time to write the story, and the sooner the better, your notes speak for themselves. Let's take a look at some of our hypothetical interviews and how we would begin the articles:

"Level of stewardship during summer is always low," John Smith, finance chairman, said this week, "and the July finance report reflects this situation."

"Easter without musical alleluias is like death without resurrection." So says our Minister of Music, Carlton Brown.

"More than 30,000 adults in this city cannot read or write," Mrs. J. Thomas Carpenter, member of Grace Church and Literacy Council officer, commented to us this week about illiteracy and the seriousness of the problem here and across the nation.

If you have never written an interview story in your life, you can master it with an A-B-C formula.

A. **Introductory quotations (the stage setters).**
B. **Identification of the speaker with his "credentials."**
C. **The local church tie-in or peg (how can we help?).**

Warning Signals: Editor's Alert

Inflammatory statements, errors, judgmental comments. We all make these at times but we would not appreciate seeing them in print. Much of the opposition to being interviewed or quoted stems from fears of inappropriate or ill-advised remarks being attributed, in print, to the speaker. As an editor, observe these warning signals:

Inconsistencies
Inaccuracies
Obscurity
Damaging comments
Negativism

Another conversation with the author can lead to a positive statement rather than a negative one, probably even more challenging than the original. It may take a few minutes longer to clear up a misunderstanding about content but the price in time is a small one to pay for a clear, informative article that adds to our life together.

The Book Review

God's Psychiatry
by Charles L. Allen
Published by Fleming H. Revell Co., in 1976.

Find faith and become a happier and more effective person. In *God's Psychiatry* the author finds the means of this achievement in the four best-known passages of the Bible:

The Twenty-third Psalm
The Ten Commandments
The Lord's Prayer
The Beatitudes

The author keynotes the use of the Bible in the application of the Twenty-third Psalm:

The Twenty-third Psalm is a pattern of thinking, and when a mind becomes saturated with it, a new way of thinking and a new life are the result. It contains only 118 words. One could memorize it in a short time. In fact, most of us already know it. But its power is not in memorizing the words, but rather in thinking the thoughts. The power of this psalm lies in the fact

that it represents a positive, hopeful, faith approach to life.

How to Get Your Children to Do What You Want Them to Do
by Park Wood and Bernard Schwartz
Published by Prentice-Hall Inc. in 1977.

The authors begin by describing what they regard as the three major parental pitfalls. One: parents are not always sure what they want their children to do. Two: parents are often mistaken in viewing their children as unable to control themselves or to act differently. And three: parents think they are telling their children to do something when in fact they fall short of being clear, direct, and effective. The authors offer step-by-step instructions on how parents can put into practice the method outlined in the book.

The approach is a positive one. It is concerned more with what parents do right than with what they do wrong. What this book does is help parents understand what it is they are doing when they are effective, so that they can extend that approach to the situations which are causing them difficulties.

The Secret Self
by Orlo Strunk, Jr.
Published by Abingdon Press in 1976.

In this life-affirming book, the author offers inspiration and hope to everyone who seeks personal development and sensitivity to the full range of life values.

Dr. Strunk, a professional psychologist, does not deny the value of group activities and therapies designed to help people express themselves, but he believes that we each have a private, even secret self that is not for public display. He maintains that the current emphasis on being public in all things overlooks the importance of this personal and private area, knowledge of which is essential for growth and maturity. Dr. Strunk starts from the premise that life is more a mystery, an adventure to be lived, than a series of problems to be solved. The suggested guidelines to self-discovery make an exciting venture into the "uncovering" of the secret self within us all.

As editor of a church publication, you read all of it, you probably write most of it . . . but do you listen?

Graceful writing blends motion and sound. It's

affirmative and it moves. Listen to your publication. What do you hear? Religious writers most often are plagued by one of the three Ps, the pedantic, the pontifical, the pious. We have put them all in one paragraph:

> The committee on church worship, having studied the articles of the 1972 convention, will, pending final arrangements, meet with members of the congregation who would like this glorious experience of learning more about our blessed liturgical inheritance.

Here are some other sounds:

> It was a simply marvelous dinner and the ladies went out of their way in decorating the room and in cooking and serving the meal.
> It was too bad that more of you did not avail yourself of the wonderful opportunity to hear Brother Jones speak.
> If we can't arrive in time, we should really question our own commitment . . . .

All such sounds, from superlatives of praise to scoldings in print, make for dreary reading, and though a writer may feel better for sounding off, little more than that is usually accomplished. Alternatives to superlatives and scoldings are facts, even from a personal view, which speak to all readers.

> Spring flowers, yellow checked tablecloths, and fried chicken changed Fellowship Hall into a country dining room thanks to members of the women's organization who served the general membership meeting. . . .

> Brother J. T. Jones, district superintendent, who is known as an outstanding speaker, lived up to that reputation here Friday when he spoke to us on decision making.

> The service will begin promptly at 8 a.m. with the processional and opening prayers. It is hoped that we all can arrive in time to participate from the beginning.

To those admonitions you received in English composition (and contained in any standard reference on writing), we add a few more.

- Use active rather than passive verbs.

    yes   The congregation met to consider building.

    no   A meeting was called to consider the possibility of a building program.

- Use words in common usage.

    yes   We will start at the agreed time even though some will surely be late.

    no   The propensity for tardiness multiplies as we continue to adjust the time for late arrivals.

- Be not repetitious.

    yes   In the event of rain, we will picnic in Fellowship Hall.

    no   In the event that inclement weather and rain does not permit us to picnic out-doors, we will hold the covered dish supper in Fellowship Hall.

- Judge not, but describe, describe, describe.

    yes   *Women of the Bible,* Martha Chapter's narrative dramatization, received a standing ovation when it was presented again Tuesday at General Meeting.

    no   That excellent program on the Women of the Bible given by Martha Chapter was beautifully portrayed at General Meeting Tuesday.

The Sentence

A sentence does heavy labor.

It carries all the weight of thought, ponderously at times it seems. It may, in fact, be so slow that we leave it before it completes its task, especially if it takes too many turns or becomes involved in some intricate byway.

A sentence goes cleanly to its mark, if direct.

It may, as the Word, be sharper than any two-edged sword, piercing to the division of soul and spirit, of joints and marrow. The Word is powerful.

In a magazine, sentences have room to stretch and expand. The usual church publication occupies little space and is easily overpowered with too much type. Do your sentences insist on all the room?

Sentences are the foundation of a refreshing publication even if they begin with pen and ink.

PUBLICATION CONTENT

Where to Begin

From the Calendar
meetings
events
special services
the liturgical year

From Church Records
births
weddings
deaths
transfers

Prayer Lists
the hospitalized
the sick

Reports of Leadership
minutes of board or vestry meetings
committee findings
the budget and financial statements
the church school

Denominational Publications and the Press
ecumenical happenings
news from the regional and national church and
its leadership

Books and Films of Note
reviewed by minister, member of the
congregation, editor

Class Study Guides—Christian Education Resources
commentaries for the whole congregation

The Community and the Church
involvement of church membership
projects and programs of note
community needs

Scheduling the Story

Every publication, whether weekly or monthly, needs a content schedule. The more comprehensive monthly might schedule all of these articles in one issue; for the weekly the articles must be divided into continuous features (such as the calendar and prayer list) and those scheduled from time to time.

Content:
1. A lead article by pastor, priest, or leading layperson.
2. Report on the previous meeting of the elders or board with special attention when needed to stewardship, evangelism, elections.
3. News of organizations and special groups from presidents or leaders.
4. Short biographies of men and women in key church roles.
5. A special series on Christian symbols with illustration.
6. A question and answer column (When a loved one dies? What is a prophet? Why go to church?)
7. A church calendar (a daily listing of events either by week or month).
8. A prayer list (those in the hospital or for whom special prayers are offered).
9. A section especially for youth. (One church we know offers a children's corner with puzzles or coloring art on the premise that youngsters are an important part of all the church does and that readership needs early encouragement.)

Regular features, as in the example of the children's corner, can serve a specialized readership, supply information in an attractive capsule form or provide continuous coverage. Before deciding to departmentalize, however, weigh these two factors: how much space is already devoted to standing features, and does it permit "play" of the news according to its importance to the entire readership. It's easy to get locked in to a standing feature long after it ceases to merit the space or attention, and too many standardized offerings may in time reduce a publication to categorized columns rather than articles directed to the membership as a whole.

Format

"In the beginning. . . ."

In the Genesis account of creation, God set life into motion, and within the process, He decreed all that was necessary for its continuation. Though complete, it was only a beginning.

Anyone who works with a church publication is involved in a creative process. A few decisions in the beginning, and the publication takes shape. The format serves as the publication's framework, housing facts, information, spiritual guidance, prayers, and praise to the Lord. Format is not sacred; it requires review. Is it time to make a change? Time to issue a monthly publication along with a single-page weekly?

Time to change the heading? Time to use a different size paper?

What's involved in arriving at the format for a publication? A preliminary decision concerns frequency of publication based on the material which must be included. From there decide on:

1. The size of the paper and how it will be folded for reading and mailing.
2. The preprinted headings for the top of page one, for mailing information on the back page, and for any standing features (staff box, schedule of services).

Later, we fill in other details of layout, more flexible than these initial decisions in which artist, printer, and editor participate.

What's in a Size?

What size paper will you use and how will it be folded? If you have ever struggled to remove a staple from a wad of paper without destroying the contents, you will appreciate the thought that goes into this one decision. An 8-½ by 11 size paper or legal size (8-½ by 14) may simply be printed front and back or it may be turned lengthwise and folded in half to produce a four-page publication. The resulting 5 by 8-½ or 7 by 8-½ handles easily without stapling and provides flexibility in layout for either mimeographing or printing.

Decisions about size go hand-in-hand with printing method. If church resources afford, and this means both in money and professional talents, the church's major publication may be a newspaper in tabloid size (about 16 by 11-½) or a slick paper magazine.

In some towns, a printing firm will "co-op" a church publication. A member church will have total use of page one of a newspaper-style publication with the inside pages devoted to advertising and general religious news common to all. Such a system makes "publishing a newspaper" feasible for even modest size churches with little or no experience in the field.

The more sophisticated publications require time in production, so other factors in addition to cost are to be considered in the final choice. Most churches rely on the mimeograph or a quick printing method utilizing office typewriters with interchangeable type. It's even possible to print a monthly "magazine" with mimeograph or quick printing, and here a staple does work to hold the folded pages together book style. Again, by turning that 8-½ by 11 or legal size paper sideways and folding, you have served the reader with an easier to handle publication.

What's in a Name?

"And Adam gave names to them all. . . ."

A name identifies in the singular and the generic. Within the name are all associations that have ever been and that may be—a name can be prophetic.

The church publication may be called *The Bulletin, The Newsletter, The Leaflet,* but it is also *The Star, The Light, The Standard, The Evangel, The Epistle, The Tidings.* A descriptive name encompasses the church's mission or message, relates to the church's name, or both.

The name becomes a standard part of the publication and for that reason it's worth the extra time and possible cost to develop a standing heading or mast for the publication. Since it will be used for many issues to come, work with an artist to design an attractive heading, not only because of aesthetics but to improve readability. Work with the printer. He will help you select type sizes in proportion to the art.

Avoid elaborate ideas. The connection of the art to the publication and the church should be obvious. Oversized sketches of church buildings can swallow valuable space on the page.

The heading may be reduced in size and preprinted on paper that will later be run through the mimeograph, or copies may be made for paste-up on the final layout for printing. Artistically, the heading should dominate the page, but it does not necessarily follow that it should take up most of the space. Neither should it be so small that it is relatively insignificant.

Christian Symbols and Illustrative Art

Let a book on Christian symbolism be your companion in planning the identifying art or logo on the heading of your publication.

Consider:
- the fish
- the lamb
- the shepherd's crook
- the dove
- the winged man
- the lion
- the butterfly
- a shield
- a cross
- the eagle
- the ox
- keys
- the tools of carpentry
- a cup
- a net

Stylize the form. Modernize. Keep it simple with a minimum of lines. The artist will probably need to use a ruling pen with waterproof black ink on heavy bond drawing paper.

Heading Design for Readability

- Does your heading provide information without clutter?
- In addition to the name of the publication, does the heading also give the name of the church? Is there provision for volume number and date?
- Have you limited the variety of type styles (no more than two preferably)?
- Do you have art work or a logo that helps to identify the publication with the church?
- Is the art in proportion to the type so that one does not obscure the other?
- Does your heading occupy roughly a fourth or a third of your page?

If all these questions bring a positive answer, your heading design most likely rates a high score on readability. If you have a negative answer, review the question and look again at your heading. Is there something you can eliminate or change for the better?

Checklist for Your Visit with the Printer

Do your preprinted materials include:
1. A heading with the name of the publication and appropriate art?
2. The name, address, and telephone number of the church?
3. The pastor's name?
4. Necessary mailing statements (i.e., bulk mailing permit number, entered as second class mail at . . .)?
5. Schedule of services, listing of ministry, or other standard forms?
6. Other possible art work (that symbol used on page one can be reduced in size and used by the return address. That sports column could have a preprinted heading.)

Make-Up: Another Chance to Improve Readability

The publication is named; the format selected, the preprinting readied, the articles prepared and given a priority rating for the pages. The typist puts the master or stencil in the machine and starts to work on the publication as you will finally read it.

But wait a minute! There's something missing in this picture. It is the layout or make-up of the page, the step which individualizes each edition and insures that there will be space for all necessary copy.

When the typist places a line between articles to separate them, he or she is even without realizing it performing a "make-up" function. Many of these decisions are passed along: the size of the margins, the placement of the duty roster or the calendar, the use of a line to divide the page—and repeated year after year. Ideally, each edition offers a variety of make-up choices from headline style to story placement. After a few editions, many of these choices become automatic. A single type-face typewriter obviously offers fewer possibilities than a multiple element electric typewriter, and the limits of the reproduction process also must be observed. But let's take a look at some make-up devices, their use and abuse.

Are you in the habit of letting articles run on and over, down one page, over to the next, and so on until all material is used? Stop! Look at each page as a whole new picture with its own layout. Look at the bottom of the page. Is there a make-up technique that would help here? Could the article be spread double-column with a bigger headline? A small drawing to the side? If an article must be continued, indicate it, use a notation: Cont'd on page 3. Cont'd from page 1. Repeat some part of the original heading: The Pastor Says (Cont'd from page 1).

Variety in make-up helps solve other problems. "I've already read that" can become a state of mind for the next edition as well as the last. For this reason some churches change the color of their paper from issue to issue, using different shades of a pale colored stock. Another change that can be "built in" is in the style and placement of the heading. Does it always need to be horizontal? Can it be sometimes abbreviated?

Art Work and Photos

One of the most effective illustrations in reading material to be found today can be seen in the art work of the Bible translation, *Good News for Modern Man*. The black-and-white drawings are lines that suggest rather than detail. It's a good example to remember when thinking about the church bulletin or newsletter because of the simplicity of the art and the absolute contrast of black line to white paper. Whether working on stencil or master or some other duplicating process, there must be contrast.

If your publication contains no art, research some of the talents in the congregation. There is usually at least one person who, with stylus or pen, can draw illustrations that may be used during the year.

Several firms now produce art work on stencils or masters which can be ordered from their catalogs for use in religious publications. Book stores and art shops may contain other possibilities, particularly if you can paste the art directly on the page for reproduction.

Experts Say:

LINE LENGTH, WHITE SPACE, HEADINGS

AFFECT READABILITY WITH ANY PRINTING

Make-up or typograph experts say that typewritten lines or lines of any printing have minimum and maximun lengths for greater readability.

A typewritten line should not exceed five or six inches, and the smaller the type, the shorter the line. Of course, you have to observe a minimum length also. If you have less than a three-inch line, chances are you won't have more than two or three words on it.

NOTE

Although boxes may be used to underscore or give contrast to page design, one of the most overworked elements of church newsletters is the simple line.

WHITE SPACE
CLEAR SPACE

White space works far more efficiently to divide the articles on the page, and even columns.

Think how simple it is to skip one more line rather than drawing or typing in a rule for a cut-off. Lines can be distracting.

TOO MANY TYPE FACES CAUSE

PROBLEMS: KEEP HEADINGS SIMPLE

Keep Headlines Together
Separated from Story
by White Space

Even when using a single type in lower case and capitals, it is possible to achieve variety in headlines. Although script makes an interesting contrast, use it sparingly as it is difficult to read in large blocks of type. Condensed type is another style of type good in limited quantity but hard to read in a mass. Sans serif types have stood the test of time for ease in reading.

Light greys and colors will not come through, but any clearly defined drawing in black and white will work.

Adapt the art to your needs, particularly if you are using mail-order packets of illustrations. Use only a portion of the art at a time. Perhaps the printed verse can be used for a heading. Perhaps only the picture of the staff, of the lamb, or of the cross. Don't let art work float alone. Place it close enough to the material it illustrates so that the relationship is obvious; under the arm of the heading allowing equal white space around, or wrapped on three sides by the body of the story. Select art that does relate even if it's written into the story: a picture of flowers with a story which begins—"Our bouquet of the month goes to the people who. . . ."

A church we know uses childhood snapshots of their leaders (the photo is identified on another page) as a regular feature. The uses of photographs are many and, though there may be some added cost to convert them for use in printing, this can be taken into account in budgeting for publication expense.

Through planning, it's possible to use photographs even with very basic mimeograph equipment. The photos can be preprinted on the paper with the stencil copy planned around it. A black-and-white photograph with sharp contrast will print best. Since it may be reduced in size, subject matter must be large enough to stand out plainly.

Church Bulletins: Evaluation

To summarize and to offer a means of evaluating your publication, consult this listing of criteria. With each major category counting 20 points, how close to 100 do you come? Encourage regular evaluation by editorial staff, communications group, the church members. Let a church school class discuss this rating and the church paper as a starter. Make evaluation a regular activity.

1. *General Appearance*
   Good readable type.
   Not crowded.
   Headlines not too big or too small for the page.
   Good reproduction.

2. *Writing*
   Brief, succinct.
   As many facts as needed.
   Accurate, with correct names (first and last) given.
   Style consistency (adopt one and stick to it).

3. *Content*
   Calendar or bulletin on events of the week or month.
   News of people, deaths, births, weddings.
   Report from the elders/board/vestry.
   Financial report when warranted.
   Editorial comment from people, ministers, leaders.
   Information about regional/national church.
   Relevant activities in the community: comment or news or both.
   Youth column.
   Sunday school department or some kind of regular church school reporting.
   School reporting.
   In-depth discussion of important matters.
   Items from other publications.
   Book and movie reviews and/or rating.
   Excerpts from sermon.

4. *Illustrations*
   Line drawings to introduce columns or highlight stories.
   Photographs: Are they of good contrast, composition and focus? In other words, are they of a quality worth using?

5. Is all space in bulletin used?

CHAPTER FOUR

The Mailing:
Administrative Ministry

Sending out an announcement about a special event?
Mailing the weekly bulletin?
Addressing the congregation through personal letter?

The times and occasions for sending church materials through the mail are many and continuous. How long ago was it that your church mailing list was revised? With the expense of postage and with the greater expense of returned mail, one of the little recognized ministries of church administration is in the organization of mailing procedures. At the same time that one or two people need to assume responsibility for church mailing, many people need to be responsive to keeping the mailing lists current and effective.

Church mailings are its means to evangelize, to pastor, to care. People who leave the congregation are not beyond this concern, and in a highly mobile society a church mailing may serve as one of its most effective Christian witnesses. Hasty deletions of names (they are no longer members here) is as inappropriate a gesture as failure to add new names.

A periodic review of the mailing list is a necessity. The services of one or two long-time members may be invaluable at this point, but by all means expand "the reviewers" to include more than the staff. Members of the congregation (perhaps as a class or group) may be asked to review the list or sections of it for corrections and to suggest other names.

Using the church's wall to tell the story is an effective communications method.

Newcomers receive a complete church information packet in a handsome folder . . . like this.

Even small churches may need a coded mailing list (i.e., send all materials, send only newsletter, mailings for the press or media). If using the addressograph, plates may be sectioned according to description (member, former member, clergy, other churches of the denomination, interdenominational) and the master list may be coded. When using plates, it's helpful to have a master listing of the mailing easily duplicated for review. Duplicated labels (available in various colors and sizes and easily affixed) are a mailing convenience and a little more costly if machines for addressing are on hand.

RESOURCES FOR COMMUNICATION

A special file in the church office labeled *Communications* helps anyone get the word out, whether a once-a-year event chairperson or a full-fledged communications group.

Such a file would contain:

- An up-to-date list of media, contact people, phone numbers, deadlines, any special information that would help place church news as to department or program.
- A current church membership roster.
- A calendar of the year's events and names of people in charge.
- Copies of articles that have been sent to the media and the published stories.
- Copies of any query letters sent to the press with response and *any* communication from the church to the media and vice versa.
- A collection of biographies of key people in the church.
- A collection of photos, especially "mug" shots

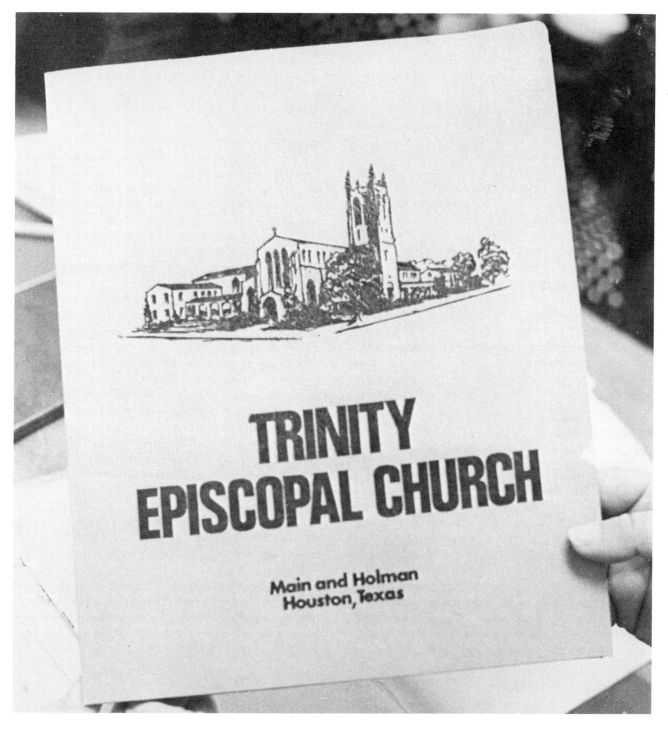

(heads only) of key people (photos should be dated). Photos should be black-and-white glossy prints.

- Background information on the church, including not only the church history but also updated sheets on current happenings: involvement in a community program, a missionary effort, a national project in which the local church partici-

pates or in which there are local implications.
- Collection of ideas for future stories about the church.

As important as organizing the file is notifying the congregation of its existence and encouraging people to use it. Any communications with the media would be a matter of common record and helpful to all.

Welcome Packet:
Introduction to Your Church

A dime-store school folder can be the wrapping for a relatively simple and inexpensive way to introduce your church to a new acquaintance.

On one side of the folder insert:

A letter of introduction *from* the clergy and a letter of introduction *to* the clergy (thumbnail biographies in order).

The church directory.

A copy of the latest church publication.

Other booklets of helpful information.

On the other side, on paper of staggered size so that page titles are clearly visible, insert:

Schedule of Services.

Church School Information.

Other Christian Education Programs.

Organizations of the Church.

Leadership Roster.

Community Involvements.

The brightly colored folder may be imprinted with the church name and address. The staggered sheets of paper may have coordinated colors. They should be updated regularly.

Reference Sheet:
Goodwill Gesture for the Media

A denominational spelling, phonetic pronunciation, and reference sheet for media people, particularly those working on newspapers and magazines, is an appreciated goodwill gesture on the part of the church. It need not be an expensive project. It can help to assure the clarity and accuracy of the church's message in print.

Some of the most often used words and phrases, including titles, should be in the list. Reporters often don't know what to call clergy—Mr., Ms., Father, the Reverend—or how to refer to a member of the clergy—as a minister, preacher, pastor, priest, or deacon. How are members of the hierarchy, if there be one, addressed? What is the usual second reference? What is the home of the minister called: parsonage, vicarage, rectory, manse? How are people in monastic orders referred to? What are the various rites of the church called? For example, in one of the apostolic churches such a list could include Baptism, Confirmation, Holy Communion, Consecration, with a brief definition of each.

Capitalization of specific terms such as the books of the Bible, names of denominations, theological terms, such as Nativity, Last Supper, Day of Judgment, are frequently confusing to news people. Some are at a loss as to how to write biblical references—(Matthew 26:12). Of course, old timers on the religious news desk, often by trial and error, have arrived at a reasonable degree of expertise on denominational language. But there is a good deal of employment turnover among reporters of religion. The church may be the only resource for indoctrinating a newcomer into the mysteries of its particular language.

Preparing such a reference booklet would be a useful project for a Church School class learning about various denominations or for a newcomers group in a particular church concentrating on its own denominational lore. Such a group could work with the communications committee on production and distribution. This would also be a good crossover project to take on with other churches. Helping educate the news media in a noncritical way may not only avert disagreement later on but can also solidify a mutually beneficial relationship.

Phonetic pronunciation of some of the more difficult names could be included in the back of the booklet for the convenience of radio and TV people.

The project could be done with the church's duplicating facilities or by photocopy. The pages could be stapled in booklet form for use as a convenient hand-held reference. A cover of a distinctive color would help the work to be readily identifiable and assure its maximum use.

CHAPTER FIVE

Interviewing: A Service for the Media

There are times when nothing will do but a personal interview.

The local news media may want

- to get into the personal views of a new minister or key staff member of the church.
- to get answers to some of the "why" questions surrounding an achievement of a church member.
- to get behind the scenes of an organization or project.
- to get the real story about a controversial figure.
- to capture the unique flavor of a person's individual expression.
- to get another side to an important question.

Interviewing is a little like playing basketball. If you are in top physical shape and well trained, if the floor is good and your shoes are brand new, and if the opponents do what you hope they'll do, you may get the ball into the basket a few times.

You won't always hit home in an interview no matter how carefully you plan. Somewhere along the line you will lose your sense of direction or the destination. Your interviewee will block the way, either inadvertently or deliberately. You will find yourself listening to a speech or sermon, or you will be overwhelmed by single-syllable remarks.

But if you can ask questions without self consciousness, if you enjoy conversing with people, if you like to dig into a subject, you can develop another tool, unique in that it can help communicate the church in a very special and valuable way.

An interview can bring out facts that might be buried in a news story or feature. An interviewer can describe a path which will lead to a particular goal. An interviewer can discover and form a story which might never have been brought out with ordinary information-getting techniques.

Can a person who has never interviewed conduct a successful interview? Emphatically, yes!

Here are some easy ground rules for one who has never tried.

1. Get as much as possible of the person's obvious background in hand through a request for a routine biographical sketch. Don't waste time gathering these kinds of facts in an interview.

2. Take notes, obviously, but not as if you are trying to hide the fact that you are writing. Ask that she spell names, repeat dates or place names if you aren't sure about them. Be sure to number your pages as you write.

3. Back up your note-taking with a tape recorder. It is dangerous to rely solely on the recorder; they have been known to bite the hand that feeds them. And even if the tape is good, the notes will save time by helping you determine which segments of the tape you want to hear.

4. Transcribe notes as quickly as possible after the interview; certainly not more than twenty-four hours afterwards, and preferably within three hours. The human memory is very tricky. Intervening data can lessen your grip on the interview facts. If you use key words in note-taking, you will be able to flash in from memory—if you don't wait too long.

5. Prepare for the interview. Decide what point or points you wish to make.

6. Set out a few key questions. Work them into the interview as it progresses rather than firing them all off as early broadsides.

7. Be flexible. Don't hold to your line of questioning relentlessly, particularly if some avenue infinitely more fascinating has developed. Be willing to be led astray.

There are two kinds of difficult people to interview and there are a number of gradations of the two. One is the inarticulate person, the other, one who "runneth off at the mouth."

Cure for the first:

Avoid yes or no questions. Put the question to her so that she has to answer. Presuppose something with which you know she will take issue. "May I assume that . . ." is a good ploy. "Then do I understand you to say that . . ." is a useful indirect lead. Also, "I hope I haven't misunderstood you but would you mind clarifying . . ."

Keep your ear tuned to what turns her on. If she repeatedly shies away from a line of questioning, drop it, even though it may be choice.

Intersperse your questions—particularly if things get tense— with some gentle personal references or comments of approbation: "You really did a great job on . . ." or, "You said you had a child. Is she showing any signs of following in your footsteps?"

Don't let an interview go on too long. At some point accept that you have obtained all you are going to get. At the wind-up, you might gather up your papers, put the cap on your pen and make other visible signs that you have what you need.

Cure for the second:

Get your particular question in by saying, "I know this is a different subject, but . . ." or, "If I may take a slightly different tack . . ." or, "Could you relate that to . . . ?" These may short-circuit the monologue.

Don't let the interview ramble for a long period. Keep gently bringing it back into the home court.

If you make your visible sign that the interview, as far as you are concerned, is over, and he still hasn't let you get to your point or shown any sign of winding down, there is little you can do. But you can, at least, at the last open moment get something going by saying, "I'd like to ask just one (or two) quick questions." Pack in whatever you can. Or, "Now to wrap it up would you say that . . ." If she consents or if she disagrees, you have arrive at some of her thinking on the subject; and that is what you came for.

THE PRESS CONFERENCE: WHEN AND HOW

The call, "Mr. President . . . Mr. President . . ." has over the last two decades become familiar to viewers of American TV. Under the leadership of Dwight D. Eisenhower, the press conference became an accepted avenue for getting important news and presidential opinion to the nation. The American public loved it, conversed ceaselessly about it, examined it minutely not only for content but for style. It was obvious by the time John F. Kennedy had honed it to a fine peak of showmanship, that it was here to stay.

The press conference, good or bad, has become an institution, not only for politics but for science, business, and other professional communities as well. Its value is that it gives a specific time for knowledgable communicators to ask questions, the answers to which might not be readily available under other circumstances. It is a tool for getting at the facts. It can be a sensitive political instrument which provides not only information but a portrayal of personality. At every level, it seems a good way to get broad exposure for information of general interest.

Press conferences are undertaken by public relations representatives as a means for getting their clients into the most media in the shortest possible time. They are used to expose specialists involved in newsworthy projects to the communications media of large metropolitan areas. They are used to announce new projects, to offer insight into controversial subject areas in which the holder of the conference might have particular expertise.

Is the press conference of any use to the church? That question might be answered by another. Does the church ever have important statements to make about itself, its growth, its programs, or its concern with humanity that warrant a special effort to get the word out? The press conference should not be dismissed as a mere attempt to "get publicity." It is in fact a professional technique for making certain kinds of information available to the public. For several reasons a church might consider holding a press conference:

1. It could be a time-saving device for busy people of national stature who may briefly be visiting a city.

2. It could be a means for communicating the viewpoints of a local clergymember or well-known layperson who is taking an active role in some program of significance to a metropolitan area.

3. It could help get out information on some model program of the church such as educational, evangelical, or social action; or some development of unique tools or techniques in dealing

with people. When the innovation has had some exposure to the public already, there may be a number of unanswered questions about the program which the press would like to put to acknowledged leaders.

4. It could help launch a major building program of some kind—new downtown church, low cost housing project, camp and conference center, or school. In 1976, when a large Houston Baptist congregation decided to move out of the downtown area and build a new suburban church complex, the building plans, design details, and rationale were revealed at a press conference.

The press conference says to the media: "We are extending to you the opportunity (and courtesy) of meeting with someone of potential news value in a candid and open atmosphere. We are interested in getting our story out and of making your job easier. We want you to be free to ask anything you wish."

How is it done? Can anyone do it? Is it complicated, a project that requires the guidance of a paid specialist? Could a small congregation—if it felt the need—successfully put on such a conference?

Good relationships with the media—a trust situation built up over a period of time—of course, make it easier to draw attendance for a press conference. Press people who are continually besieged by demands on their time will be apt to attend an event headed by someone whose judgment they know to be sound. But if a press conference—and even press relations—represents totally uncharted waters, it is still possible to hold one and have it accomplish what you had in mind. You want to be reasonably sure the situation—the material or person you are going to communicate—warrants a general gathering of media representatives. In other words, it's not something you do every day but, when you have good reason, you do with confidence and in a professional manner.

Here are some things to keep in mind:

1. Get the consent of the person around whom the conference will revolve far ahead of time (at least three weeks if possible, so you may prepare back-up material and alert the media).

2. Send an advance notice to the media about what you intend to do. Enclose a biography and picture of the person. Include a news story about his or her appearance in your city, which covers the title of the talk.

3. Invite religious news editors if the story is strictly church-centered, but also ask the city editor if the story has further implications. (You might also want the women's editor, medical editor, political editor, or other news specialist.)

4. Set a convenient place to hold the conference—the church's parish hall or large meeting room, a hotel or motel meeting room, an office conference room.

5. Try to set the time for the convenience of TV reporters so that they can make their evening news deadline. Check with the stations as to the best time for them.

6. The day before the conference call all those invited to remind them and see if they plan to come.

7. Have someone heading up the conference to be responsible for its conduct, to introduce the speaker, announce the ground rules, if any, and to cut off the conference at the time specified. The conference might take anywhere from forty-five minutes to two hours depending on the time of the speaker and the number of press.

How elaborate should the conference be?

A place, some chairs, a table, some advance biographical and basic information about the speaker's expertise—these are the main requirements. The conference is a business, not a social event. Everyone's time is severely limited.

A press reception is more elaborate, calling for refreshments, a more ornate panoply of printed materials, perhaps even a press kit in a specially designed and printed folder. A press reception might be indicated when a church is unveiling drawings for a major building project, planning a venture into a new and significant program of works affecting an entire city, or one that calls for a high degree of ecumenical cooperation. Visual displays might be included—mock-up or model, drawings, photographs, even a film or slide show (brief). Invitations are usually sent out in advance, with telephone follow-up. The format may be a brief speech of welcome by a principal in the project, followed by two or three brief statements by others involved, and an open question time.

An informal press event may be a substitute for a conference and may be preferable if the visitor has limited time, if there are not that many area media interested in him as a newsmaker, and if the field of expertise lends itself to a more involved dissertation. This can be set up by contacting a specific reporter at the time a news release is sent out announcing the visitor's coming to the city. If several press people wish to interview, specific times could be set up so that there is no overlapping and each reporter can get his own story. Good coverage usually results. Or interviews could be sandwiched into the visitor's schedule at random hours when he has a brief respite from his duties.

A press conference following a speech or public event is a natural and is the easiest to set up. Find a room in the auditorium or conference center where the press may gather with the speaker after the talk. In this way questions posed by the speech can be answered. The press is likely to be present already for the talk. This kind of courtesy will enable them to get yet another dimension if they wish to do so. Such a conference is usually informal but it still should be guided by someone representing the church so that it will not become too lengthy, and to insure that all press people have an equal chance to question.

Some press conference myths:

A press conference will automatically get you off the church page onto the front page. Not so. You may have a better chance but it depends on the speaker's stature and subject. Why do you want to get off the church page anyway? Good and faithful readers follow you there. You run the risk of getting lost in the news section.

A press conference can be controlled so that there is practically no risk of unfavorable or embarrassing questions being asked. Obviously this is not true as you are given no chance to screen questions. Your opening remarks can, however, set the scene, define the parameters in which the conference will be conducted. The advance material, the speech being responded to, or the circumstances in which the guest appears in your city, are other elements in setting up that definition. Of course, if things get particularly tough, the guest can always refuse to respond to a particular question. At that time he or she can redefine—or you, as leader of the conference, can—the reason he or she is there. Most press representatives are much more interested in getting at the truth than in embarrassing the guest. It is well to be certain that your guest is comfortable under the give and take of incisive interchange before you make conference arrangements. Particularly is this true in the event that he represents a viewpoint in a project or program thought to be controversial. If he has never been exposed to the media before, you might give him some insight—which, hopefully, you have—on the special interests and personalities of your local press people. If you are familiar with their work at all, you will know what type of questioning your guest will probably be exposed to and you can prepare him.

A press conference should involve only secular media. Not so. Ask editors of denominational publications and of major church newsletters. Ask people involved in editing ecumenical bulletins and newspapers if the subject would be of interest to them. Here is where your list of publications—hopefully kept up to date—can be used handily.

In the ordinary routine of communicating the church, the subject of the press conference is one which will surface only at rare times. It is well to know some of the ground rules and to be able to look at the benefits from such a project so that when the time comes a decision can be made in a relaxed and confident frame of mind.

CHAPTER SIX

The Survey: Is Anybody Out There?

From time to time, it's important for a church to know: Are we communicating? To whom are we communicating? What are we communicating? The poll or survey is a tool, both within the church membership and outside of the church, to link sender and receiver in the communicative process.

The poll may be a means in itself of expressing interest, of saying we, the church, want to know about you. Based on the Christian ethic to establish communication where separation exists and to determine needs, the poll becomes a means for self-appraisal and evaluation.

Early in his experiences, Henry Ward Beecher, the great nineteenth-century preacher, discovered that he failed when his purpose was to produce good sermons, however scholarly, factual, and earnest. His success came as he looked to the needs of his audience. He told the seminarians at Yale:"Take men as it has pleased God to make them; and let your preaching, so far as it concerns the selection of material, and the mode and method by which you are presenting the truth, follow the wants of the persons themselves, and not simply the measure of your own minds.''*

Recently a major denomination in Texas earmarked more than a million dollars for a multimedia evangelistic effort, but not one part was planned until a marketing research organization had reported on its survey of 60 cities and more than 600 people. In the findings, people described their concerns as loneliness, purposelessness, distrust, suspicion. Tabulations also indicated their interest in the church. "The survey gave us the direction we needed," one official commented later, "for a series of testimonials from actors and businessmen, sports figures, housewives, who spoke of their problems and their changed lives in Christ."

Whether scientific sampling or simply a straw poll, the survey or questionnaire can provide a working base of information for clergy and laity, in New Testament terms the "royal priesthood" of the church.

A survey team from a church in a midwestern city stationed themselves in a nearby major shopping center in a project they considered one of the most valuable ever initiated. The purpose of the survey was to determine if the nearby public was aware of the church and how they viewed it. The questions asked:

Have you ever heard of this church?

If you do know of it, how did you hear about it?
  Friend?
  Newspaper ad?
  Radio announcement?
  Other?

Have you ever been to this church?

Do you know people who attend?

What one word would you use to describe it?

What one program of this church do you think is particularly good?

What do you think this church could do to reach more people?

In another part of the country, a church takes a look at itself through an intensive visitation and surveying campaign. A data sheet keeps track of the answers:

Name and address _____

Number in family _____

Special church interests _____

Prior church work or activity _____

---

*Henry Ward Beecher, *Yale Lectures on Preaching*, New York: J. B. Ford, 1972, page 56.

Has someone from the church visited you in last year? _____

Do you receive church mailings? _____

What do you think are the strengths of the church?

Its weaknesses _____

Any other remarks: _____

The data served as input for decision making for months to come, and even later provided guidance for the calling of a new minister when that occasion arose.

Scientific pollsters say we change phenomena by measuring them and that an interview acts as a catalyst. In this way, a church survey would not only measure the effectiveness of its program, it would also be an instrument for change. Along the same lines, the poll when publicized and discussed acts as a reinforcing agent, reason enough to take its potential seriously. Certainly, polls can be important to the church, whether in communications or Christian Education or as a body to evaluate what is being done, to increase awareness and sensitivity to others, to set directions for the future.

PROCEDURES

Procedures for a survey or poll:

1. Define the purpose in simple terms.

   Does this church need a communications effort for evangelism?

2. Determine the means.

   A survey to be conducted by the communications committee.

3. Determine the method.

   _____telephone poll
   _____mailed questionnaire
   _____person-to-person interview

4. Write the questions.

   (An explanation of the purpose or reason for the poll should precede any questions.)

5. Plan for tabulation and interpretation of the results.

Maximum number of questions to hold interest of respondents is about ten, and usually five or six are sufficient to determine opinions or seek input. It's helpful to all to formulate simple questions that can be answered briefly or in a short period of time.

Questions can be factual and should be neutral:
The church communications committee sponsored two projects this year as evangelistic efforts, on radio and in the press. Do you think efforts should be made to increase the number next year?

Questions may be multiple choice:

> Did you hear the 7 A.M. Sunday broadcasts on KARE held during March?
>
> Never
> One Sunday
> Two Sundays
> Three Sundays
> All of them

Questions may indicate intensity:

> How do you feel about the church's radio presentation on abortion?
>
> Strongly object
> Object
> Have no opinion
> Support
> Support wholeheartedly

Questions may ask why:

> Why did you object to or support the presentation?

When it's time to analyze the returns and tabulate, be sure to record any pertinent observations or comments. Let a group work with interpreting and discussing the conclusions. Then, it may be time to disseminate the information—to a governing body, to the church membership, and perhaps even to the press. From the experience of other church pollsters, it may well be at this point that survey participants find themselves with a strengthened sense of the corporateness of church life and a new grasp of the church's mission.

CHAPTER SEVEN

Cassettes:
The Pervasive
Voice

Recently the communication arm of the National Council of Churches of Christ in the USA (NCCC) reported that over the past six years the retail sales of audio tape equipment has exceeded seven billion dollars with eighty percent of United States homes now possessing cassette, eight-track or reel-to-reel tape players. The figures quoted were from the International Tape Association in Los Angeles which is a clearinghouse of information concerning the fast growing audio industry. The NCCC report went on to state that prerecorded audio cassette programs exist in all sectors of society and that the production of religious cassette programs is a rapidly proliferating industry.

There is no doubt that audio tape is a permanent part of the communication/education scene in America. Here is an electronic medium that has been enthusiastically embraced by churches of every denomination and size. Our world today, says Roy Lloyd writing in *NCCC Chronicles*, is "literally wired for sound." He submits as evidence of this the tremendous quantities of cassette recorders, stereo and quadrophonic systems being sold every day—the sound systems that have become so much a part of both our public and private worlds, from the piped-in sound in our elevators to the playback units eminently visible in their plexiglass cubicles in school language classes and libraries.

Whole tape ministries, in churches large and small, continue to grow. The simplicity of the medium, its power for pulling people together, as an enabler for sharing, as an educational tool, are all factors in the increase of its use as a means of spreading the Word of the Lord and the work of His people.

Bringing Paul Tournier, or Billy Graham into a

150-member church, asking them to preach a sermon or lead a discussion group would, obviously, not be feasible. Yet these same religious leaders are available to that church through the medium of tape at nominal cost. Messages from all of them and many more of their caliber are available through national tape libraries or sales outlets, either on loan for a nominal rental fee or for sale. There is also a free world out there of tape material. Obtaining it is simply a matter of placing a tape recording device of some nature in the hands of a willing church member who can push a button, and then let him or her attend a live event featuring material of interest. Or he could use the recorder to pick up selected material from radio or television. In either situation he or she would need only the simplest of equipment to transcribe the words of the great and bring them back into the church. Lest we seem to be advocating free-wheeling taping of any event without restriction, let us hasten to state there are some programs—particularly involving music—where, for obvious reasons, you cannot get permission to tape. The artists make a good part of their living through tape sales, so anything that might be interpreted as an act of piracy would not be looked at kindly. You can also not copy for public use many professionally made tapes including study tape series. If you are in doubt about any particular tape, ask the publisher or check with the producers of the program you wish to attend and tape.

Sound cassette making can become an interesting and important ministry for the church. Cassette tapes can provide the nucleus for a variety of educational experiences. They are excellent vehicles for self-criticism, as in the case of minister studying his sermon or a church school class looking back at its discussion.

Cassettes do a much larger job than merely transferring sound from one situation to another. Tape recordings are builders of bonds between churches—ecumenical, intradenominational, large church with small church, churches of different ethnic traditions. Tapes are links between shut-ins and their churches, overseas workers with home base, different age groups in the church with one another, the church with community and vice versa.

If tapes are to be considered an alternative to ventures into another medium, or a possible first step into the very large and complex world of electronic communication equipment, consider two major advantages: (1) tape is inexpensive, (2) tape is easy to produce. Another consideration shared by the electronic media is that tape emphasizes the group experience. By its nature it brings people together. Reading is a solitary exercise. Even when people read and talk about what they have read, they are often trying ideas out on a single other person so that the relationship remains a matter of one-to-one. When a tape is played, people become united in listening. They are at the same point in listening at the same time. They have all heard the same thing, often in different ways, with different reactions. Discussion following heightens the group's sense of itself, its unity and variety. The same tape played again for another group may produce totally different responses. Two or more groups hearing the tape, recording their feelings, sharing them with others can get a tremendous sense of being opened up, of sharing new frontiers of understanding with others in the church. Tape reaches people in a far more personal way than does printed material.

Those who may object in some way to being taped in discussion or conversation will, after one or two such exercises in which others participate, usually find their objections disappear. Prior to the taping sessions, it may be well to deal directly with such objections, which usually range from "My voice sounds awful, I can't stand to listen to it." to "I'm afraid I might say something I'd want to take back." If the nature of the discussion is such that the group agrees that the tape should not be shared—a rare instance, most certainly—then the tape can be erased by running it back again on "record" in a silent room or by recording other material over it.

An advantage that tape shares with radio is that it does not require the attention of more than one of the senses. It is possible to listen while doing other things. Youngsters in a church school class can draw while they listen. Some people like to knit or do needlepoint. One man confessed that he liked to doodle while

listening and, indeed, it helped his concentration. Some people like to take notes for discussion later on. Tape gives this freedom. The freedom itself is relaxing. The nature of tape also allows it to be previewed easily. A taped discussion series may be heard prior to class use by the leader or instructor. With a cassette player in the car or a small portable variety it is possible to listen to Sunday's lesson while driving across the freeway on Friday. The leader is thus in an excellent position to direct the group, having achieved an earlier insight into what the material proposes.

A number of factors determine whether or not a tape is being used to good advantage within the congregation.

1. Does it involve the whole church?
2. Does it represent crossover between groups?
3. Does it bring in ideas that strengthen faith, expand knowledge of the church and Christ's teachings, help people to understand themselves?
4. Is it entered into responsibly, used as a serious study medium rather than as entertainment or diversion?
5. Is it a growth medium for those who participate and, ideally, for the whole church? Does it help people know one another as they are?
6. Is it a part of the ongoing life of the church rather than a device to beef up interest in a dwindling church school or save a group whose members have lost interest?

It is well for tape, initially, to be talked about as a program of ministry, since it is likely to involve purchase of some equipment or to seek the loan of equipment from members. The whole church should be made aware of why those who favor tape think it is good and why everyone will be expected to participate in the program. It must be clear what the program will be, how much equipment will be needed, how all can share in it, and what its advantages are.

A tape study may be introduced by way of the Department of Christian Education. Learning programs may be purchased or rented from a variety of sources. Many of these are prominently advertised in religious publications and may be ordered by mail or are available through local bookstores. Large churches in your city may have tape libraries with subjects of interest. Universities or public libraries may have tapes featuring readings of classics or modern works of interest to the church, and these may be available on loan for a nominal fee. Often denominational offices, either regional or national, have tapes available or can give information on where they may be obtained.

Audio equipment adequate to reproduce the many fine tapes being professionally made will add richness to the church's life.

A congregation serious about using tape may want to set up its own tape library. This will have the effect of bringing tape usage into the core of church life. You might start with the Christian Education learning tapes. After the series has concluded, these might be made available to other groups of the church or to individuals. A benefit of this approach is that it could have the effect of expanding interest in church school. Certainly there can be no harm in having as many members as possible aware of what the church school is studying, even though they may not choose to be active participants.

When tape sharing is done through a church-sponsored tape library, an important level of validity and identity accrues to the tape concept. It becomes much more than one person asking another if he or she can borrow a tape for the weekend. The process of checking the tape out of the church's stocks makes you a part of a program that has the qualities of being both popular and permanent.

The requirements for operating a tape library are nominal. You need some kind of storage unit (a large cardboard box clearly marked will probably do for a while, but later you may need a file cabinet). The tapes should be kept in clear plastic snap-shut containers, all of them clearly marked as to name, church's name and address, and any coding that may be helpful in keeping track. A notebook to record transactions would also be useful, as would a set of rules clearly

posted in the vicinity of the tape storage unit. The tape library may be a part of the church library or it may be entirely separate. One or several persons may be designated to be responsible for tape check-out and check-in or you may have the honor system where people sign for the tapes themselves. You may want to make a tape recorder, as well as tapes, available for rent. You can presuppose that most of your members will have their own tape recorders. The over twenty-fives will probably own cassette units, but the younger members of the congregation will likely have eight-track decks. But don't try eight-track tapes or reel tape as a standard form for your library. Standardize on cassettes. They are easier to transport, are practically foolproof, and can be indexed and stored handily.

Set a time limit for use: two weeks, with a fine after that. Notify people who are overdue by mail or phone. You might charge for initial rental, more for past due rental. This requires some bookkeeping but it is hardly more than nominal. The important thing is to keep up with what is in and out. Set up a waiting list. Notify people when their tape is in. This can be done through the church newsletter. A number of churches run a "tapes in" corner: "Charles Brown, Pat Rogers, the tape you signed for is in. Bob Green, yours is overdue. Please return." A side benefit to this approach is that the whole church becomes aware of the availability of tapes and the process by which they may be borrowed.

OTHER ASPECTS OF A TAPE MINISTRY

To bring the worship service to shut-ins. To bring messages from the minister to people who are sick or in need of consolation. To say hello to people who have moved away. To keep up with overseas work. To share thoughts or programs with other churches. To inform community groups of the work of your church. To provide a critique vehicle for the minister or others. To provide a creative experience for youth or others who might want to use tape to develop "radio drama" or a mixed music/sound presentation for the church.

To bring the whole church into an awareness of the tape ministry, you might use the parish bulletin to critique new tapes, pass tapes from one age or special interest group to another with appended comments. Or, if you have a parish library, you may make up tent cards for point-of-display messages telling about new tapes. A tent card is simply a piece of cardboard folded in the middle with a message on both sides. Some churches have broadened their tape ministry by sharing with schools, different ethnic groups, different denominations, governmental bodies. This is not just a matter of taping their activities for their own use but of sharing tapes they have enjoyed and found useful.

Preparation of a church's own study guides for tapes is another facet of the tape ministry which can be exciting and challenging. For this a small group of people are required to meet together and study the tape. What is most interesting about it? What are the main points? What would spark response, positive or negative. You might examine professional study guides for help. You might only want to prepare a main point sheet which everyone can have in hand while listening to the tape, a list of questions that will be asked afterwards, a directed comment sheet where the audience can list reactions as the tape progresses.

Tape as a Stewardship Tool

Expressions of the principles of stewardship exist in much of the content of tapes gathered by the church's tape committee, librarian, or whoever may be asked to review and order tapes. Such material may be utilized specifically for stewardship by noting on a piece of paper exactly where it is located on the tape. Running a tape on a recorder equipped with a counter will facilitate location. After a number of such messages have been located, it is easy to make an entire tape focused on stewardship. The picked-up segments may be bridged by comments from the stewardship chairman, the minister, or others in the program. The stewardship program could be a tape in which every part of the church is represented.

The most impressive such presentation we know of featured young people talking about what the church meant to them; a group of older people expressing how much they depended on the services and worship of the church, some upper echelon executives talking about their experience with tithing. It concluded with some remarks by the minister. A tape of this type should not be long. Fifteen minutes is a good deal of listening, particularly since the electronic medium inserts no spontaneous moments of drama, alters no facial expression, makes no gestures. Lengthy tapes are generally productive of little more than boredom. One way to add a dimension to the tape is to show slides or present other visual materials during the course of the sound. This requires other kinds of expertise such as synchronization, and it may also call for some additional equipment if synchronization is critical. (See chapter eight.)

Tape as Vacation School Booster

We have heard taped programs prepared for this purpose beautifully and professionally done, with mixers to bring in appropriate music and the sounds of children happily at their play-work. A tape visit to this year's vacation church school can be a strong promotional tool to stimulate interest in next year's version.

Uses of tape to stimulate interest in church outreach are without number. Comments from members of a family or organization being aided, snippets from missionaries overseas, all can serve to inform the church of its own work and bring in fresh voices. This is not to say a tape of this type should be a recitation of expressions of gratitude—far from it. Glimpses into the lives of others removed from the congregation can enrich members of the church as well as develop support for outside works.

Tapes are excellent for use in explaining how a program works. In connection with organizational charts or chalk-board presentations, the tape can give a definitive glimpse into the work of another organization, or explain a facet of its work.

But why tape? Why not bring in living representatives to talk? Here are tape's advantages: (1) Tape is dependable. People sometimes don't show, charge money, or can't be pinned down to a specific date. (2) Tape timing is reliable. A fifteen minute tape runs for fifteen minutes. People know what to expect and they can relax as they listen. Tapes can be edited or can follow a script so that they present just the information that is needed. Live speakers can bumble and stumble, imparting little data. They can talk forever. They can be boring. It is possible to have some control over a tape; very litte over a speaker who is an invited guest.

A strong urge to emote, to participate in drama, exists in the hearts of many of us. Tape can be helpful in developing such talents, satisfying such urges. "Re-create old radio" was the theme for one church's tape celebration. Different groups got together and did segments of long-ago radio favorites: *Jack Armstrong, Lights Out, Ma Perkins*. It was a highlight at a church supper. A small drama can be presented on tape. It can be acted out in pantomime (very effective) or with slides. Such participation helps people become familiar with microphones, quelling any fear they may have of the sinister implement—useful talent to have if the church is considering going into one of the electronic media. The more people work with tape the closer they come to achieving victory with language—succinct statements, arresting expression, tight development of subject. Voice control and variation are also necessary skills which tape helps to develop.

To begin your tape ministry, it is first advisable to consult your talent and equipment bank to determine what is available. A committee meeting to look at the whole concept of a tape ministry assures that this will be a responsible part of church life rather than a one-time thrust. A committee, in its initial stage, might meet to discuss ways in which tape can be useful in the church. There will be two broad categories: ongoing programs and special events; several subcategories: Christian Education, stewardship, exchange, youth. A chart can be developed. Index cards outlining possibilities can be set up and filed. The first venture into tape should be a substantial one. A sound presentation in more ways than one! You could, as in the case of slide photography, audition and make an event of the auditioning. You could have a catalogue of church people's voices, identified with their names and program areas. This would be handy to have in preparing a pageant, church drama, one act play or other similar program.

The committee will also want to discuss with department heads the possible purchase of teaching tapes and their uses. Contact could be made with companies which prepare such programs. Also, contact can be made with companies which sell tapes in multiple lots. The price break could be considerable, the quality superior to many over-the-counter brands.

A subgroup, with the purpose of bringing into the church tapes of outstanding programs or speeches, could be set up. "There are two great programs on television this weekend. One is a message by a noted theologian; the other a layperson speaking on a subject of wide concern. Bob, will you tape the theologian? And Barbara, can you do the other? And a noted African missionary is to be in town this week. Who can attend that and tape it? A Gospel singing group? We need that too." There are all kinds of opportunities: great speakers, music, debate, drama. With a tape recorder and some willing people this wealth of talent can be yours. Your subcommittee might want to function as an editing group later, listening to the tapes and editing them for brevity. They may add music or some local comments and for this may bring in other departments of the church. Once the tape library is going and the indexing system operative, you will want to publicize the library and the tape programs. Here, indeed, is a major ministry for the church. Smaller churches can take all or any part of it and adapt it to their particular situation. There is no reason why tape should not figure prominently in the life of all churches regardless of size.

EQUIPMENT

Tape recorders are as many and varied as makes and models of automobiles. Plain and fancy. Extended capability. Simple. What do you need? First answer to that is: make use of what is available, i.e., what your congregation owns and is willing to have used in the tape pool. Or buy at least one for the church; it will be a good investment. In buying a tape recorder, simple and sturdy is best. One that uses either batteries or alternating current. A condenser mike. Preferably a machine with a counter and automatic record level. A fairly good-sized one that lies flat or stands up. Avoid tiny recorders however fascinating they seem to be; they can be spirited away more easily, they are prone to fall off tables or out of pockets. They are also more expensive. A good tape recorder can be acquired for less than $50. You may want to put $25 into a separate speaker with a jack that allows your tape recorder to play back through the speaker. Most inexpensive recorders are perfectly reliable for recording but haven't much speaker power. Play back through the speaker of a television set, the speaker of a quality sound system such as that of a stereo record player, eight-track, or good tape player. For this purpose you will need a cord with the proper connecting tie-ins to the system. The unit you use to produce your final tape should, for best reproduction, be one equipped with tone controls and balancing so that the very best possible sound may be achieved.

Making the Final Tape

Is it enough merely to play back the sound you have picked up from your seat three rows back in the auditorium where Billy Graham spoke? If the quality is all right, the tape not too long, and there is not a great deal of disruptive miscellaneous sound, you may feel this is good enough to use. But you may want to edit, for length if nothing else. You may also want to add music or some discussion comments. You may want to mix these in with the speaker's voice. How is this accomplished?

Several ways. The expensive way would be to use a mixer, which costs anywhere from $50 to $150. This gives you the capability of putting in additional sound where you want it in one operation. It is simply an input unit with accommodation for two or more microphones. There is no mystery. You bring in mike one which is feeding in music; with master volume control you fade it out, at the same time fading in your next mike which is picking up the main part of the tape, the speech. The third mike brings in your comments or some formal statement from time to time indicating a break for coffee or introducing discussion.

Without a mixer it is still possible to add other sounds professionally. You need a separate tape unit, record player, or radio to provide music or other comment. For live comment your copy unit must be hooked to a live mike with a hand-held, on-off switch.

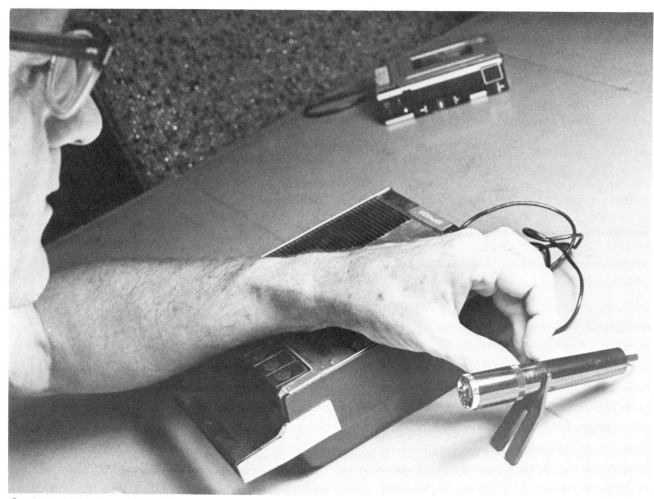

One kind of microphone for use in interviewing.

You may want to take your speech directly off the playback; you can do this by plugging your patch cord into "ear" on the unit that is playing the tape and into "in line" on the recording unit. Watch your volume needle on your recorder to achieve the best balance throughout. If the needle persistently swings off scale or swings wildly from low to high, manipulate your receiving volume, which preferably has tone controls as well as volume control. When the needle holds fairly steadily, you will have a good balance of tone. Don't record at the top volume level when you are taking sound directly off a radio, television, record player, or tape player. The sound is likely to be distorted and you will have very little range for controlling it.

A pause control on your unit is helpful. This will stop the tape while you set up for bringing in sound from another source (radio or stereo). It's a lot easier and smoother to push a pause button then to stop a recording operation in the usual two-button way, or even to click a mike switch.

A person working your music source equipment will switch on when you point to him, and you can bring it in smoothly by gradually turning your volume down on the tape being recorded and up on the music. Hold on the music for a few seconds to establish what it is, then let it go under again as the tape volume increases. Music is also a good bridge for bringing in a second voice or an announcement or pause period.

To edit tape it is good to listen through at least once, keeping your eye on the counter numbers and making notes as to what you want to take out. Then make a copy tape, picking up only what you want, and leaving out the rest by using your pause button as the original tape runs. To rearrange segments, do the same thing, keeping accurate records on your counter so you will know in just what sequence you want the final tape to be.

Cassette duplications can be made in the manner described above or by running them on tape recorder number one with a mike and letting unit two pick up off the mike. Danger here is loss of quality (unless you

CASSETTES: THE PERVASIVE VOICE

have a first-class microphone) and picking up additional background noises such as telephones, door bells, etc. You need studio conditions for this type of recording. Try doing it in a closet if you aren't bothered by claustrophobia. But this is doing it the hard way. Using the direct record system you can go off and leave it running with just an occasional check back to see that the tape is not hung up. Note: You are much, much safer to use quality tapes. Also shorter tapes—30 to 90 minutes—have less tendency to snag and break than 120-minute tapes. But none are absolutely fool proof. However, a big advantage is that you can "copy" while talking to someone, watching TV, going about business as usual.

There are duplicating services. Most are relatively inexpensive; you pay for the tape and a few cents more for the service (something like 10¢ each). Cassette duplicators start at around $350 and go on up to $1,000, but they are a good investment if you are planning a major tape ministry—sharing with other groups and churches. It may pay for itself, considering the lost cost of good blanks bought in volume. Be sure about the copyright on all tapes you plan to duplicate.

The quality of the cassette, as stated before, should be top of the line. It will hold up better under use, will give you better sound, less grind, hiss, and whir. Some tapes can be disassembled by unfastening three or four small screws. They can be untangled and a bad part cut out for reuse. Most tapes, however, are moulded plastic and if they tangle or break, the best thing to do is throw them away and start over. Chromium oxide tapes are of excellent quality and some recorders have optional accommodation for them. They aren't necessary for average use. Get high-density low-noise tapes. Keep your recorder head clean by running a head cleaner through occasionally. The new cobalt energized cassettes add to the high end frequency response, and you get more brilliant recordings. A Dolby noise reducer on your copying unit is helpful. It cuts down tape hiss. Keep your tapes in dust proof boxes. The soft plastic see-through containers are excellent. You can read the name of the tape through the box and it protects the tape in shipping and handling.

There are companies that will upon arrangement record an entire conference or convention for you. They make masters and professional duplicates. They will usually set up a booth to promote and sell copies at the conference. They will also sell tapes by mail.

There are magazines devoted to sound and tape recording. There are tape sections in several of the leading photography magazines. The library has numbers of books on specifics of tape recording if you want to go into it more deeply. New equipment and modifications pop up all the time but a good standard machine that is rugged and gets reasonable care from its users is probably all you will need unless you plan to develop major tape programs for sharing with other churches or groups. We have not gone into detail on other kinds of recording approaches—reel-to-reel or eight-track. Eight-track blanks are available and some units have recording capability. They are not as easy to handle as cassettes, and they are larger and more susceptible to malfunction. Reel-to-reel with good equipment will produce the best quality of all but, again, you have the probable scarcity of equipment and the difficulty in handling the tape. This can be equated with the difficulty of handling roll film or an open reel typewriter ribbon as opposed to a cartridge film or ribbon. It's easier, more compact, and less can go awry. Besides, more people have cassette recorders.

Some Things to Remember in Recording "in the Field"

When you go to an auditorium or to a conference to tape, follow a check list:

1. Do I have fresh batteries (alkaline energizers are recommended)? Are my nickel cads charged? If I plan to use AC do I have an extension cord?
2. Do I have enough tapes?
3. Do I have a pen handy to label tapes as they are completed? (It is a good idea to have side one and side two already marked, then all you have to do is append a brief description; indeed, you can also do this in advance.)

Put the date on your tape and, if it is a conference where the speaker might address the group more than once, or if it is a tape of proceedings, the time. "Spring Conference, Side One, May 18, Friday A.M." would be a typical listing. Side Two might be: "Spring Conference, May 18, Friday noon to 3 P.M." To this you might add a highlight: "Discussion on Ethics: Shepherd, Brown." If you are taking notes you might write down a key note or two and in the margin "Taped Side One, Friday A.M." This brings you right into the tape if you are planning to present a written report for your church newsletter.

Try to get in a good position—front row, facing mikes. An empty chair next to you would be handy for placing your microphone if it's not built in. Have a mike stand so you don't have to hand-hold. Don't move the recorder or mike around during recording. Don't add conversation of your own during the session. Cut your volume down during applause—or

When you have guest speakers, be sure the audio is the best you can provide.
Taping the event may give you an excellent study tool.

off to save tape. Use identifying keys if you need them . . . "Dr. Simon, Dean Smith, Chairman of the Ethics Committee." This may be necessary if speakers are not identified. Or you can take notes on identities and if your tape has a counter, list the number on the counter where they begin to speak. "Dr. Simon 425." These kinds of identifying notes help cut down on tape search later on.

Experience in the field will help you develop shortcuts of your own. The more you use your equipment the more relaxed you will be with it. It will not be very long before you have admitted tape into your life and the life of your church as a valuable vehicle for sharing.

Rich experiences become available through the use of audio equipment, and sometimes the whole program comes about accidentally or as the result of some single event. A larger church we were told about had on its rolls a church school teacher who because of the requirements of his second- and third-grade classes could not attend adult church school. They were at that time discussing "Death and Dying," and the teacher wished fervently that he could participate or at least hear what was being said. He requested that the sessions be taped so that he might have access to

them. Some adults who had to be away from class for several weeks decided they too wanted copies of the tapes. Some shut-ins were interested, and at least two people whose eyesight was poor and who were having difficulty keeping up with the printed study sheets, applauded the idea of having tapes available. Now, as a matter of course, tapes of all adult class presentations are made available through the church library. Each tape can be checked out for a period of two weeks. A cassette player can also be checked out for the same length of time. The tape ministry of this church has expanded now to include tapes by visiting speakers at their own and other churches, some professional tapes by leaders in certain fields, including two theologians and a seminary dean. The ministry has added a richness to the life of the church which may be only the beginning. A committee is now functioning to decide if there are other ways tape can be used and shared.

A tape ministry, once begun, will surely grow. That is the nature of such a program. People are thirsting for words that express faith, answer questions, dispel doubt, stimulate thoughtful response. To be able to feel that one has been given access to high levels of theological thought as well as practical guidelines for human living is at once exciting and satisfying.

CHAPTER EIGHT

Slides: A Simple Visual Adventure

The mention of words and pictures quite spontaneously suggests both film and television. There remains a third medium which embodies the two elements—the slide-sound presentation.

Though only under special circumstances can slide-sound be classified as a mass medium, it is effective in reaching reasonably large numbers of people and it lends itself to communicating substance of wide appeal as well as of a highly specialized nature.

As with all other media which play dual roles as carriers of information both within and outside of the church, slide-sound carries with it the responsibility to use it in a Christian way. Because both the taking and viewing of still photographs are unquestionably personal experiences, the need to be mindful of this dictum is even more urgent. A single slide viewed over a period of 10 to 20 seconds can have substantial impact on the viewer that would be far greater than any single frame in a movie or scene in a television show.

Slide-sound utilizes simple equipment to present an audiovisual message. It is possible to enter this field at a number of levels and the difference in the final result will be obvious only to the skilled professional.

Here is a medium in which you can have mechanical simplicity with authenticity of material. You can go into it as deeply as you wish, assured that even at the very beginning level you can achieve an effective result. It is possible to invest in an array of impressive equipment including wide screens, special effect projector lenses, slide titling equipment, illuminators, rear screens, dissolve units, and mixers. The investment in such extras can run anywhere from $25 to well over $2,000. Most of it is simple to operate, but it is not all required.

When the church has developed its talent and equipment bank (see chapter one, Talent Bank) and has it working, equipment may cease to be a problem. At best it may only be necessary to fill in gaps created when certain items are not available from church members. There should be a mention here about being aware of members who own equipment. They may move while you are midway in a project. It is possible they might leave the equipment to the church as a farewell gift. This possibility should not be overlooked!

A SLIDE SHOW

While film may be the church's ultimate objective and it may not want to settle for less (young people are often particularly anxious to jump over the intermediate step), slides are an excellent learning ground for people who want to become comfortable with equipment, mechanics, and composition. Some churches do a good visual job with posters and an occasional live presentation. But the beauty of slide-sound is that it can be repeated, expanded, shown before a variety of groups in their own habitats. Slide-sound programs require as many or as few people as you wish to involve. Slides, like film, carry a high degree of authority and authenticity.

Slides may be used in the classroom as a teaching tool, as a promotional medium for a stewardship program, as a means of introducing the church to newcomers. In fact, an investment in one set of slides can provide material for numerous uses in the church. And copies are cheap, so you can have several sets simultaneously circulating.

What Should a Slide Show Be?

At the simple end of the scale a slide-sound presentation should be a pleasant, effective storytelling mechanism which points out briefly that which you want people to recall.

Slide-sound can be made as complex as a Cecil B. De Mille spectacular. It is possible, for example, to have four projectors running simultaneously with dissolves and mixed sound. It can be blended with film strips, live action, live music, other add-ons. It can be the cornerstone of a bigger, more involved presentation or it can stand alone.

What Should a Slide Show Not Be?

- A miscellaneous collection of pretty slides.
- A series of slides shot exactly the same distance from the camera.
- A group of pictures with no central purpose.
- A group of pictures of poor quality, under or over exposed or out of focus.
- A group of pictures not related to the tape or live narration.

At its worst, a slide-sound show might bore some people. At its best, it will present a message that will be viewed with deep attention and carry a high degree of recall.

The Beginning, The Middle, and Some Pitfalls Between

You can start at the bottom of the scale with an inexpensive pocket type camera. Our preference would be to use a camera of 35mm film size, though others are also acceptable. The problem with the smaller format (110) is that it requires special projection equipment as does the larger size (2-¼ by 2-¼). It is helpful to select a camera with a good lens, particularly if its lenses are not interchangeable.

Good lenses, sensitive film, computerized processing, all tend to eliminate many of the problems that dogged photographers back in early color days. Many people offer an inexpensive camera as an excuse for poor photography, but this is not necessarily the case. Had they held the camera properly, taken notice of light, inserted the film correctly, and had the lens cap off, they could have produced slides of acceptable quality. Conversely, a good (expensive) camera does not mean a good slide. There has to be a happy marriage of a certain amount of care and expertise with a certain level of performance of equipment. It is well to get thoroughly acquainted with your camera before beginning to shoot. A photographer of our acquaintance recommends an extensive dry run with a new camera and open instruction book, going through every phase of its action, changing lenses, checking out all the refinements, without film.

Fortunately you don't have to be exactly on target these days. There is a good deal of latitude in modern film. You can be an f-stop off when shooting most color film and still expect to get a usable product. With black-and-white film you can be off by two f-stops (exposure factor expressed in amount of light that passes through the lens). With color there is the added trickery of film suitable for use in daylight only, or in artificial light only (tungsten). Misuse will give you outdoor blues with tungsten film, indoor yellows with daylight. The way to get around these problems is to read the film instructions carefully. If it says daylight, shoot in daylight.

Read flash or electronic strobe instructions. If instructions indicate you need a filter under certain conditions, get the filter or change the conditions. And be sure you start out shooting film suitable for slides; that is, color positive film recognizable by the word "chrome" at the end (Ektachrome, Kodachrome, Anscochrome, Fujichrome). If the film says "color" at the end, it can't be used for slides unless it is one of the types (Kodak 5254 or 5247 are two) that specifically states it is both positive and negative. Otherwise you will have nice album prints but no slides. With slide film and camera you have basic tools for slide-sound.

More Tools—The Slide Part

A good part of your slide show will be done "on location." You will take people doing the things you plan to talk about in the show. There are many time and labor savers, many gadgets that are helpful in the process. None of them are necessary, and most are expensive.

1. *The illuminator or slide sorter.* This is essentially a rack made of translucent plastic with a 60-watt bulb behind it on which you place 40 or more slides at a time. This enables you to study your slides, make comparisons, gang them into order. It is a good tool by which a group can study slides and critique them simultaneously. An illuminator can be made from scrap materials by a do-it-yourselfer, or one can be purchased for from $12–$15.

2. *Slide title set.* A U-film kit costs about $2.50 and consists of enough special slide film material and

mounts to make 22 title slides. The U-film will take impressions by felt-tip pen, colored pencil, or even typewriter. It is possible to make your own title slides using those clear ones obtained when you boo-booed in shooting (everybody has one or two of these stashed away somewhere). Gather them in and then write or draw on them with fine felt pen or grease pencil. You can also buy professional title type, dry transfer, which allows you to place letters on the slide and with a rub of the finger transfer it to the surface. Cost is less than $3 per sheet.

3. *Number tabs:* These come in different colors for keying sets of slides and are affixed to the edge of the slide.

4. *Slide titling labels:* Useful for keeping track at a glance. Most are color coded so you can move slides from one show to another and retrieve them when you are repeating the original show.

5. *Mounts:* You can buy heat-seal mounts which can be sealed with a warm iron or with a heat-seal mounting press (cost about $20). Or you can order plastic mounts that snap shut for about twice the cost of the cardboard heat-seal type. You won't be dickering with mounts unless you tell the processor to return your film unmounted in a strip. Then you cut and mount each slide—save money. Good if you plan to do a lot of slides and also affords a good project for a group that wants to get into it.

6. *Special effects:* You can order mounts cut in rectangles, ovals, stars, diamonds, and so forth. This gives you a good variety. Also you can create special color effects by sandwiching two slides in a single mount, or by sandwiching a slide and a square of transparent colored plastic. Good for moods.

7. *Copying equipment:* You may want to copy maps, pages from books, drawings. To do this, tack the material to be copied on a wall where there is good even light (you may have to add some light for balance). Put the camera on a tripod so the image will be sharp. For smaller items you may want a copy stand. If you don't want to invest in that you can rig one with a tripod and a clamp. Idea is to have the camera looking down at the copy (which is evenly lighted) and very, very steady. Copying slides is another ball game. Slide copiers are fairly expensive—up to $40. If you want lots of duplicates, for several programs, you will save money. It costs from 50¢ or more per slide to have a commercial processor duplicate.

The possibility of adding in black-and-white slides should not be overlooked. These can be made from your black-and-white (or color) prints, though it may be a bit more difficult to find someone to do this kind of processing. You can make your own simply by copying black-and-white material on color film. Mixing black-and-white and color may be indicated in situations where emphasis is desired. There is intense drama in black-and-white which can be used advantageously to make a point. You may even want to do an entire show in black-and-white.

This gives you a basic glimpse into what's needed for shooting your slides. At the back of this chapter you will find a list of manufacturers of this kind of equipment, as well as a brief list of books that will answer most questions. We want to stress simplicity throughout this chapter because we feel slide-sound is a medium that can be done easily and effectively by amateurs, and one in which mistakes can be rectified without high cost. We cannot see any reason at all why even a very small church could not consider making a slide-sound presentation sometime during the year.

PUTTING YOUR SHOW TOGETHER

Organization

The production of slide-sound should be a part of the total life of the church. It should take place throughout the year rather than approached as a one-shot, all-out-and-forget-it kind of project. A rush to go out and get slides together within a constricted time period may result in an incomplete thesis, poor quality, a garbled message. If you don't have time to ponder and discuss, you may have a group of attractive colored squares that have no relationship to the Christian faith and do not reflect the conviction either of the subject or those involved in the project. In this case the tools cannot be blamed. They are indifferent. In the hands of devoted Christian people they become powerful messengers for the Lord. Why do we make this slide show? To tell about an event in our church? To tell about our church? To be our church?

Slide-sound planning can take place at the beginning of the church's year, the time when many of the important decisions are made, the budget prepared, annual reports given. This is opportune, particularly as the project may require some budgeted funds, either expressly written into the budget or earmarked out of another budgeted category such as stewardship, Christian Education, or communication.

It is also opportune in that it may be well to consider drawing upon a full year or major part thereof for your

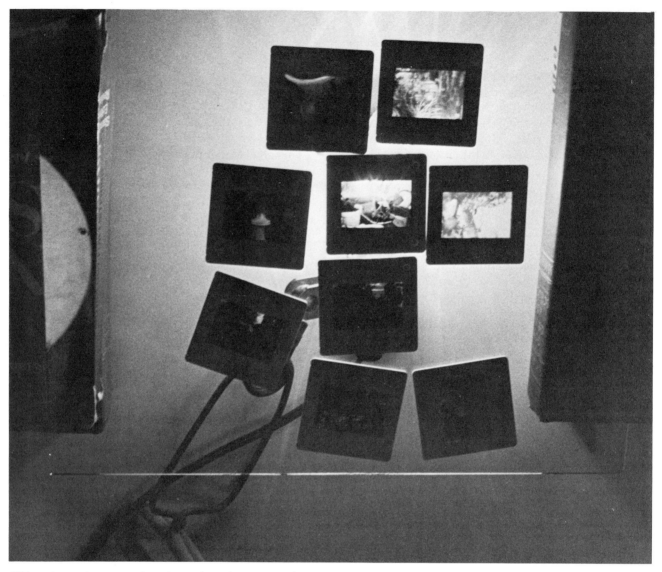

Slide sorters cost money and maybe you haven't a carpenter in the house. We put a piece of plate glass over two piles of books and set a bare bulb underneath. Be sure the bulb's wattage is not too high. You want light not heat.

slide material. Several important events in the life of the church can be documented—the slides, with identification, stored in a proper file. A year's worth of effort can provide background for a fascinating history of the church as well as useful material for a variety of purposes. Slides may be taken by persons especially assigned or by persons who own cameras and know how to use them. Ideally, an invitation to join the shooting party may go out to the whole church. It would not be amiss to offer to view slides from anyone, but always with the stipulation that the slide-sound committee has the right of editorship which includes acceptance or rejection. Giving photographic credits in all slide shows is essential and can easily be done with titling materials.

We are going to take for granted at this point that you have organized a communication committee in your church, or at least have designated a single person to hold this responsibility (see chapter two). When the communications committee meets at the beginning of the year, it may see fit to delegate responsibility for slide-sound to a representative of each department or function of the church. The Department of Christian Education's representative would thus be responsible for working with that group on planning, shooting, and taping specific activities.

As the communications committee begins to get into planning, the kinds of slides to be made—as indicated by the communication needs of the church—will begin to be obvious. Fine planning involving each department can then begin; insight will develop into how the slides can be used, how they fit into the overall communications purpose of the church. If communications has developed a theme for the year, slides can be worked easily into it.

Theme

The theme may be quite an obvious one such as the 25th anniversary of the church. Slides will be invaluable in pointing out the growth of the church, the variety of its activities, the church's growth as it relates to the growth of the community, the kinds of people it serves. Some of these photos may have to be constructed if there is no historical backlog of materials from which to draw. You may be able to copy some things—document of founding, old certificates, old photographs, and the like—but most churches tend to have large gaps in their recorded history, so you may have to improvise. With a little ingenuity you can recreate your church's entire history.

The year's theme may be outreach, community service, or simply faith as expressed in the activities of the church. We recall a church which did slide-sound around the word "miracle," using the faces of people within the church helping those outside. There was a real sense of "miracle"—the Lord working through people—in the presentation. The situation was the adoption of a Vietnamese refugee family. The church communicator meeting with the minister shared the belief that it would be good to have a "mini history" of the new relationship. There was no thought at the time—not until the first slides had been returned—of producing a "miracle" play. But the faces of the children, the expressions of joy and simple attempts at understanding, produced the message. It was clear and certain, and it stimulated a great deal of excitement throughout the church. The first photo crew was augmented by others, and a great variety of slides was obtained. At the end of six weeks the communicator and the minister, plus key members of the church, sat down with hand viewers and some 250 slides. It would have been bewildering except that the communicator had a rough script. Slides were put into stacks, each of which illustrated an area of the script. They were studied and compared. Editing required several evenings. The script was rewritten a number of times. It was timed and taped. Several voices were used on the tape. With a mixer they added some Vietnamese singing and speaking under the narration. A moving introduction was provided by the simple prayer of a young Vietnamese girl, over which a close-up of her face and some scenes of the welcoming of the family were shown. The show was very effective and served to bring others into this area of ministry. It was later loaned out to other churches and, in at least one instance, it helped a sister church to come to a decision as to whether or not to embark on a similar project. The adoption of a family (and it's done every day by churches)—whether Vietnamese, disadvantaged, tragedy-struck, or whatever—is an excellent opportunity for bringing slide-making into the life of the church.

The slide show may encompass the flow of one area of activity into another or it may be a compartmentalized attempt to tell everything about one specific area. There is a rationale for either of these approaches. Blocking out segments tends to give a thorough background to an activity and, at the same time, to give it weight. Some function overlooked in the busy life of the church may be brought to the fore. Those involved in the activity will get a strong sense of identity with it. As a tribute for unsung heroes, the slide-sound presentation is unsurpassed. Presenting the varied church in one sweep can produce a feeling of interrelationships or of people working together in faith and love. It presents all the facets of the church so they can be looked at and understood as parts of the whole. Both approaches have their place.

Involvement

Slide-sound gets many people involved. Without realizing it they become, through the medium, a part of the communication process of the church. They get an understanding of what it means. Often individuals who have seen little merit in a communication program are suddenly caught up in the challenge of slide-sound and realize they are communicators. A self-generating enthusiasm runs through the various phases of production. This phenomenon has been explained as the effect of being a part of the larger professionalism represented by the film industry. For many it is a first opportunity to experience any kind of working communication media involvement. An attitude develops and often pervades other areas of church activity. Working in a group, working on deadlines, being able to express criticism and give creative force to a project, having a showcase result which can be looked at by people known and unknown are part of the unique package which is slide or film production. Mastering equipment, the very use of which gives the recognition of professionalism, is partly responsible for the heady enthusiasm which often develops during a shooting project.

Planning

Planning meetings are essential, and it is necessary to see that the opportunity to get in on the act is made available to all those who would like to do so. Many roles are involved in the total project; there is little danger of anyone being left out. Here are some of the categories:

Photographers   Editors
Prop crew   Script writers
Scene crew   Screeners
Storyboarders   Publicists
"Actors"   Equipment committee

Set out the roles and try to match the roles with the people. Some may be disappointed. There may have to be crossover or duplication. The idea of having a time commitment to a specific project on a deadline basis may appeal to some and not to others. Your goal must be to involve as many as possible without letting the bulk of the burden fall on any individual or group.

Photographers may have to be auditioned, their work viewed, their equipment checked out. It is not necessarily a matter of weeding out the unsophisticated in favor of the person with a raft of lenses and a motor-drive 35mm camera. You might want to mix your talent, give different assignments to fit capabilities. Auditioning can be an exciting exercise, one which could have both suspense and prestige attached to it.

Prop people work at the discretion of the planners and storyboarders. They will help set up the objects which are required in the scenes. Scene people will set up the physical arrangements, such as making an appointment to use a building, determining the best area of a building or room for shooting, working with the photographer to weed out unnecessary factors from the scene. Both prop and scene crews work closely with the photographer.

Storyboarders are the initial planners for the project. They may use the familiar storyboard procedure which calls for a number of 3-by-5 cards on which ideas for the various scenes are noted. In the upper left-hand side of the card, a crude drawing of a slide to illustrate the idea may be sketched. The cards may be taped on a wall or storyboard rack, or laid on a table. Then they are juggled about until the story line being sought is achieved. Both script writers and photographers would be involved in this phase of the project.

The "actors" are, of course, those who pose for the pictures. They may be people procured on the spot, such as at a specific event. Or they may be sought in advance for set-up shots.

Editors are obviously those in on the development of the project from the initial phase to the end. They are called on to weed out what is not wanted or needed, keep pressing the quest for usable slides, revise, rewrite, work with the entire committee as the work progresses.

Script writers after the initial storyboard conference, may go off on their own to write and polish a script. They may then put it on tape, for audition, reedit, or work on synchronization during the final phases of the work.

Screeners are those responsible for setting up screenings of the work in segments as it progresses, and organizing the final phase for study and editing.

Publicists will inform the whole church and any outside bodies of what is going on, give a build-up to the showing, invite comment, organize a review.

Researchers gather background material for the narration, help track down charts, or other illustrations.

Impetus Group

Who will provide the impetus? Who will proclaim with enthusiasm that this is a great idea and let's go with it? You may want to look to an organized group already functioning at a high level of efficiency. In every church there are active people who seem to lead all the rest, who are ever ready to tackle new adventures and inquire into new approaches. In some churches it may be the youth. They are universally interested in the media, and photography is a challenge within reach. They like and admire equipment and those who use it. They have a tendency to comprehend the intricacies of equipment rapidly. The problem may be to harness their immense supply of energy, tack them down to a plan, cut through all of their many competing activities to hold them to a project schedule. Surprisingly enough, seniors are often eager to be on "that" side of the camera though they may be more shy with equipment initially. But many seniors today travel casually about the world with elaborate photography equipment and are relaxed in the milieu of the colored slide show.

The church's organized specialists—such as the Christian Education Department (includes adults), stewardship (should include young people), special events, or mission groups—might be the ones to furnish inspiration for the project.

Steps

From impetus, your group proceeds to planning which includes determining a theme for the show, a purpose, a rough script, the number of slides required,

A crude story board indicating some shots for a slide show.

equipment, props and scenes needed, and, perhaps most important of all, deadlines.

"We're going to do a slide show on the church's Mission in the Migrant Farm Workers Community. When are we going to do it? Well, we'll start now and see what we come up with. Who wants to take pictures? Say, it would be good to have it ready right before Thanksgiving! How about it?"

There is plenty wrong with that approach. In the first place you need many specific deadlines. First,

deadline for initial planning. Must be finished by the 25th. Deadline for shooting first segment (this may tie into an event or events and would have to be a block of time built around that specific). Second segment. Third and fourth segments. Four parts are manageable. If you are doing a show around a single event, obviously you won't need a four-part deadline. But if you are including several events as well as day-to-day scenes and some set-up shots, you will find this a workable procedure. And, incidentally, the working plan may not be the sequence in which the slides will be shot. You might do the end of the show first.

You will likely want to set up a chart which will be posted in some readily available place during the project. You might have someone check off with colored pen each segment as it is completed. The whole church can be involved in the progress of the project—and suspense will build. The chart will give dates on which various things are to happen. It will indicate the total time period to be consumed by the project. It is desirable that the concentrated working time not exceed three weeks if possible. People will be excited about your project but you can't hold them in that pattern too long. At some point along the way you may have to choose between deadline and some particularly interesting additional material. You will want to be flexible but not flabby.

Audition

We mentioned having an audition in order to select photographers. This can be a project for the whole church or at least that segment of it involved in the project. Set up a projector, or projectors (you can have several screenings going on at a time. Have each person desiring to participate bring in six slides he or she thinks best represents his or her work). Let properly constituted judges (they might be from outside the church) make the decision. If this is an open competition, nobody's feelings should be hurt and there should be quite a bit of prestige in having been chosen. The designation accomplished in this way will tend to generate commitment to the project, and that is essential.

The audition or an all-church slide show operated as if it were a mini film festival can be a memorable and fun occasion for the church as well as bring forth individuals who are deeply interested in making quality slides.

Established or Learning Photographers

You may not want to use established photographers at all. You may want eager beavers with bright-eyed points of view but no expertise in using a camera. Your slide project will then become a learning project, a skill-development program. You can readily set up a one-teach-one situation with an experienced photographer assigned to one or more rank amateurs, helping and guiding them through the necessary steps. Since "doing" slides does not involve processing, this would not be a long or involved procedure. The church might want to hire a local photographer to spend several class shooting assignments with the group. Or experts who are church members might volunteer. Good working bonds are established through these kinds of arrangements, an understanding of the medium, and the power and uses of film, and a commitment to a block of time.

If the one-teach-one does not work out, a series of three or four classes with one photographer doing the basics might be an alternative. Getting people to understand the importance of the project and to be comfortable with their equipment whatever it is are the main values of such a series.

Through these methods the slide show can become a part of the life of the church. Open the process up to everybody, invite the whole church to "walk through" every part of the show, ask for ideas. Emphasize the validity of using "equipment" to express faithfulness, to give the Gospel message, to help the church to its chosen work. The slide show is the sword. But those who wield it must know that it is. No one simply snaps a shutter and takes a picture. He reproduces a scene in a way as unique as that of the painter. He sees it in his own fashion, interprets it, and expresses personal feelings.

Resources

A church in which nobody knows anything about colored slides need not abandon its slide project. There are many sources of help and information in the surrounding community. Numerous, simple-to-follow guides for taking slides and creating slide shows are available at photo shops and department stores. A good reference publication is a copy of either *Modern Photography* or *Popular Photography*. Spiratone, Porters, Helix, and others are mail order photo supply houses that claim low prices on accessories, and their catalogues offer a bewildering variety that's fun to look at. You may have to ask a professional what's the best buy. Which brings us to another dependable source of help you may want to tap—your local camera store. There you will find an expert willing to talk to you, and you will be able to look at and touch the possibilities. Tell him or her what you want to do, the money you feel you have to spend, and allow them to help you see how you can get the most for your investment. If there is more than one camera store available you may want to compare notes. Your committee might want to study and discuss the information, check with the finance committee or other church authority before buying.

When You Are the Photographer

Moving out of the preparation stage—planning, organizing people, gathering equipment—you move into the shooting stage. You have a shooting schedule and a fairly good outline of what you want. You have a theme and some background on how to handle the camera, what kind of film to use and under what circumstances. You know when you will need help with flash or strobe lighting and when you can get by with daylight. You know how to read a light meter or how to translate your camera's visible data.

The mechanics—the ABCs—are not too hard to memorize and repeat in use. There are intrinsic things that are a bit harder and may require trial and error. You have to train your eye and maybe there isn't time to do enough training. So you will have to rely on some guidelines—general of course—in taking your shots.

1. *Vary the range.* Boring is the word for a slide show that is all close-ups (above the neck), medium close-ups (waist up), medium shots (full length), or distant shots. Boring also is for one where all the backgrounds are fuzzy. Have a variety but don't have it in a willy-nilly fashion. Remember that a close-up shot gives drama and emphasis and should be used to make a strong point. A child biting into an ice cream cone says something strong about the ice cream, about herself, her time of life, the world she lives in. A segment of a stained glass window with vivid light effect says something about the church's history, its role in civilization, its stability, its leadership.

2. *Vary the lighting.* A drift of sun through stained glass, light reflecting off a shiny object or plane, the soft flame of a candle, the even light of florescent bulbs, the harsh shadows of noontime—each may be used advantageously. You might want to shoot the same scene in different lights, using it as a recurrent theme shot. This can be very effective. You don't have to take many photos before you begin to notice light and its effect on the subject. The film is the paint, the camera the canvas, and the light the paintbrush. You may want to study the subject, moving it or yourself slightly, watching the effect of light on different surfaces, before you make your picture. Light can create moods and can be a strong ally in expressing what you wish to say.

3. *Be cognizant of backgrounds.* This is particularly true when taking pictures in color. You should high-point your color and not let it drown in a conglomerate background. Plain colors, active background; active design, plain background are a good rules of thumb. Don't let background distract from main action. When you become familiar with the camera you will learn how a wide open lens close-up will tend to soften and diffuse the background so that it will be a soft blur of color. You may want this effect from time to time, but

not always. In other shots you may want details of background. Ask before you shoot: Is the background (a) compatible, (b) distracting, (c) important? The background can give a picture identity—a child standing with his cotton candy before a perspective of ferris wheel, and other carnival attractions; a man leaning on a corral fence behind which is a herd of cattle.

4. *Vary the numbers.* Big groups—a procession, picnic crowd, meeting—can set the stage, give a "feel" of the event. But smaller groups generally do a better job. Big crowd shots one after the other will put people to sleep. First the crowd and then the face is better. Posed crowds—everybody looking into the camera—are the worst possible fare. A posed Sunday School graduating class sitting on the lawn is boring. The pastor congratulating two Sunday Schoolers by giving them a hug gives the feel of the event. You may have to sacrifice numbers for feel but at the same time there is no reason always to home in on the same people. Your camera should be into many groups in the church, show many faces. One or two people working on a project, laughing and talking, shot candidly, make better subjects than sixteen people lined up at a table piled with craft items they have made. Let people come alive on your beaded screen. Get their genuine selves.

5. *Vary angle.* A church shot straight on may be uninteresting, but when you get down on the ground and shoot up on the steeple, it may rise in a strange and interesting way that is more than pictorial. Don't be afraid to distort familiar things. This can add to the interest of your show as long as the distortion is planned and the whole show is not one of the things distorted.

Now we are ready to shoot an event—an all-church picnic and homecoming for which oldtimers are returning; a tree will be planted and homemade ice cream will be served. Relay races and a softball game will be offered for all ages.

Shooting Script for Slide Show

Homecoming Picnic
(Segment of Larger Show—Ten Slides
Total number of slides to shoot: 40–50
(Film is cheap. Processing is relatively so. Rerunning the picnic is impossible. Take many more slides than you actually need).

Slide One: People putting on name tags. Close-up of two people, one pinning tag on the other.
Q: What is the purpose of this slide? To establish the event, emphasize the importance of knowing names,

emphasize the friendliness of the church, introduce two people.

Slide Two: Highlight of the day—homemade ice cream. Medium shot of people waiting in line with center action (people serving) in the background. Purpose here is to show the event, give a crowd feeling.

Slide Three: Child eating ice cream. Close-up.
Purpose: Present feeling that is typical of the whole event. Homemade ice cream is "traditional," so this shot gives an implied feeling of past roots and homey-ness of the church, its values.

Slide Four: Softball or other event. Distant shot.
Purpose: Good youth activity figures in life of church throughout the year. Depicts healthy youth relationships.

Slide Five: Closeup of kid in baseball cap or with bat.
Purpose: Continuation of above. Individual expression of pleasure in event.

Slide Six: Relay race winner given ribbon.
Purpose: Friendly competition. Interrelationships between people. The joy of winning. All good statements.

Slide Seven: Minister talking to old-timers. Medium shot, maybe four people. Minister hugs one while other two look on. They hold plates of food.
Purpose: Multipurpose shot: This is a picnic. Minister is warm and friendly. Church sponsors enjoyable afternoon. Minister cares.

Slide Eight: Close-up of oldest old-timer or some significant person.
Purpose: Everyone is important in the church. People care about the church's events.

Slide Nine: Close-up of people participating in tree-planting ceremony.
Purpose: Church cares about the environment. It is a matter of pride to make church grounds look attractive.

Slide Ten: Distant shot of people gathering lawn chairs, putting them in cars, packing to go home.
Purpose: Formal end to this segment. People have come out to this event and have stayed. It was and is important to them.

This is what you aim for. You will have many more slides than these and many won't even be related to those listed. You may throw out some of the original list. You may add slides, make other changes. Some may seem to be more meaningful than these. At this critical time your committee will have to be open and flexible, cognizant of the overall purpose of the project and how each segment advances it.

THE VIEWING

Here's a whole new chapter in the program. The slides are the raw material. The projector and screen are the pasteurizers which make the slides available for consumption. Probably a third of all American families today own some kind of slide viewer. The church can probably put its hands easily on two or three. Many churches own one or more for use by various departments. You don't need the most complex viewer in order to show slides effectively. You can use the old push-pull version without harming your presentation. We've done it using a second person working with a copy of the script wherein the slide keys are marked. It's a little uneven but the audience hardly recognizes it if the quality of the slides is good.

The best viewers are carousels or cubes, either top or side loading. There are other styles of course. A good projector is not expensive (under $200) and it can be used in so many ways that no church should be without one or more.

If you are buying one now, get one with a remote control, remote reverse and forward, automatic focus so that each slide is automatically brought into focus by the machine and you don't have to rack the lens back and forth to get sharpness. This makes the show smooth and uniform. A carousel will hold from 80 to 140 slides. They come packaged for filing on a bookshelf. The normal lens on the unit you buy is probably all you will ever want.

For delving into more artistic techniques there are wide-angle and superwide-angle lenses that are excellent for rear screen projection and can fill a 40-inch screen at only four feet. There are zoom lenses for change in effect during showing. For small rooms, one of the wide-angle lenses may be indicated. Other normal lenses which can be bought separately will enable you to fill a 50–60-inch screen at short distances.

The following chart shows the focal length of the lens and the amount of screen it will fill at what footage. This is important where room space is limited. It is excellent to consult when buying equipment for classroom use and in church schools.

If you are buying a projector, it is good to have one that has an accessory outlet to accommodate a sound sync unit, programmer, dissolve control or remote extension cord. Dissolve control gives blended transitions into slides. Two projectors are aimed at one screen, both plugged into the dissolve control unit. When the cycle button is pushed, one projector picture fades out at the same time the other fades in. There is no distracting blank-out. The transition between pictures is gentle and even rather than jarring, as in the

Lens Focal Length	Screen width				
	40″	50″	60″	70″	100″
1.4″	4 ft.	5 ft.	6 ft.	7 ft.	10 ft.
3″	8 ft.	10 ft.	12 ft.	14 ft.	20 ft.
4″	10 ft.	12 ft.	14 ft.	17 ft.	24 ft.
5″	14 ft.	16 ft.	20 ft.	23 ft.	33 ft.
4–6″ zoom	11–17 ft.	13–19 ft.	18–23 ft.	19–28 ft.	24–39 ft.
7″	20 ft.	22 ft.	27 ft.	33 ft.	46 ft.
9.5″	27 ft.	30 ft.	37 ft.	44 ft.	62 ft.

case in ordinary projection. Cost of a dissolve unit is around $200.

Now, to match your sound and pictures you will want a sound synchronizer. The synchronizer is used to put a signal beep onto one track of the stereo tape while music and narrative is put onto the other track. When the tape is played back with the projector, the slides change whenever a signal beep occurs. The beep is not heard by the audience, so the automated show proceeds quietly without the need for an operator being at hand. A sound synchronizer costs somewhere between $40 and $50.

Mixers: Music is a good low background. So are authentic location sounds. You might want a sound or music theme running throughout the show, different selections for change of pace, or a repeat front and back theme.

How do you do it? The easiest way to record narration and background simultaneously is to have background sounds playing as you narrate into the same mike. You have to be careful about extraneous sound; you should use a directional mike on a stand and be placed the proper distance from it with the background music or sound dropped far enough away so that it does not override your voice narration. You might have someone else helping you so the volume can be increased to bridge segments or for special effects. You can fade music in and out by adjusting the volume of the record or tape player. Or you can turn the mike toward and then away from the sound source. Or you can feed both microphone and playback machine into a mixer that feeds into your tape recorder. You can control the volume of each source with the gain controls on the mixer. You can use monitoring headphones or make a few trial runs for balance.

With a stereo tape recorder you can record narration and background on separate tracks. You can make changes in one track without affecting both. Later you

may combine the tracks by feeding the output of both channels into a single channel on a second recorder.

A mixer could cost from $50 to $200. Most have three or four inputs so you can produce a wide range of mixed sound effects.

Alternatives (The Cheap Kind)

If you haven't the stomach for synchronized sound or dissolves, and the thought of running two or three projectors fazes you, stick adamantly to the single unit, live voice narration, or use a tape track which you have carefully timed to accommodate to the slides. As long as you are hand-running things you can keep the show's elements tied together reasonably well. Each slide should be shown for about 15 seconds, not less than 10 nor more than 20, for maximum impact. You need about 50 words maximum per slide. A good slide presentation should last from 20 to 30 minutes, no more. You can integrate it with other elements. Music to begin and end on is a good idea and can be done via your portable recorder. All slides don't need copy. Some slides should have music or no sound at all; just because you have a slide visible, don't feel obligated to tag it with 50 words.

For a cheap slide synchronizer for your tape recorder, you can buy self-adhesive metallic tabs to put on the base of the tape when you want to switch to the next slide. The tape travels on the two contacts of the synchronizer, and when the tab bridges them the projector is tripped and moves to the next slide. These range in price from $5.95 to around $12.95. Ask your camera store for more information.

For taping in the field with an inexpensive portable recorder, be sure you have fresh batteries or that your unit is fully charged. Use a quality tape that will record everything the recorder is capable of. Get in close with the microphone. Remember that most field recorders do a passable job of recording; it's their playback that's inadequate. Get a patch cord that will patch your recorder into another speaker via the ear input on your recorder. Cords and adapter jacks are not expensive and can be purchased at any sound supply store. Just tell them what you want to accomplish and they'll steer you to the proper materials.

Uses

We have mentioned in general terms the uses of a slide-sound presentation. In so doing we have not dealt with its uses as a teaching or as a promotional tool. Slide shows taken in the field can be useful in the Christian Education program because the students become a part of the process. The slide show offers an excellent opportunity to draw upon individual ingenuity as well as group brainstorming. A church school teacher decided to ask her students to film a parable. It was a team assignment, with each team composed of three students. They had two to four weeks to research their own parable. Prior to the assignment the class had been studying the biblical parables. The variety of living parables brought forth from the assignment were both interesting and inspiring. It made the students look at the concept of "parable" and at the parables of our Lord in a new and significant way. Their parable pictures were later shown to the whole church and eventually they became the nucleus of a sharing program enjoyed by other churches. The slide show was integrated with a live presentation by the young people themselves, explaining how they had accomplished their project. The class also put together a scrapbook with their thoughts and comments about the project, augmented with photos of the crew in action. The project was considered to be a high point in the church's year.

Other Educational Uses for Slide Shows:

1. Modern duplication of biblical scenes.
2. The church in action in today's world.
3. Reaching out to help others.
4. Social situations and biblical comments on them.
5. The church in the community.
6. Who needs help? An examination of different groups from which a decision might be made as to how they are asking for help.
7. Good things about the church.
8. Not so good things about the church.
9. This is how I view the church (with input from a number of groups and individuals).
10. Other ways of worship (field trips to other churches).

There are countless ways of mixing slide shows with the church school curriculum. The slide show also offers an opportunity for presenting the work of the church (Sunday) school to the whole church. Often the church seems to be a series of enclaves, none of the members of which know what the others are doing. The slide show can bridge the gap.

The slide presentation may work best with other media or as a part of a larger program. A series of slide shows which our denomination did, for example, on Africa was augmented by a "live" show of African artifacts and objects. A demonstration of the wrapping of a piece of cloth into a native dress, a display of free literature including brochures and leaflets, photocopies of articles for background information. The slide show gave the brunt of the message. It can usually be relied on to do that capably whether it is to introduce a new building campaign for the church, to give an informative view of the church's life, or to present a plea for budget support. Printed material is always a good reinforcing adjunct to the slide presentation. The printed material will recall the show to mind, giving it a second wind. A basic principle of advertising applies here: One show is not enough. Follow-up is essential.

The slide show for promotional purposes will be different in feel from one used for educational purposes. It will be more "selling," and each photograph will be carefully selected to "do" a particular job, make a specific point. If you are trying to say in a promotional show that the church needs a new building, you will want to show the following kinds of shots:

1. Crowded classrooms.
2. People sharing facilities.
3. Churches in the immediate area with good facilities.
4. Closeup of principals in the situation being interviewed or making a comment.

If the thrust of the show is that the church should provide a day school for children of the community and of the church, the shots might be:

1. Crowded public school facilities (bike rack full of bikes), children crowding at door, long line of school buses.
2. Page of textbook or workbook that needs improvement.
3. Shots of children who will be served by day school.
4. Shots of some of the people who will be involved.
5. A model or drawing of the building.
6. Shots taken in other church day schools, show-

ing advantages of this type of education (one-to-one pupil-teacher relationship, for example).

The minister may want to give the congregation a look at the hospital visitation program. The slide show would be an effective medium for doing that; it would enable one church to "visit" another. It may put the church into the center of a controversy in the community, with photos of a nursing home that renders poor services, a polluting sewer plant, trash on the streets, and the like. This requires photo journalism techniques, and sometimes the real meat of the story may be hard to get. You could also do an inspiring story about a community of handicapped people.

Symbolism may be integrated with "life" shots to underline certain points. The cross, the church door, candles, a branch of a flowering shrub, a pair of boots, some gnarled hands—all of these can be powerful and moving point-makers.

If it seems in reading this material that slides do only a shadow of the job that film can do, and the question comes to mind why do slides at all when film is so much more effective, you might consider the other side of the coin.

- Slides require less expertise.
- Equipment is cheaper and more available.
- Slides can be copied and shared readily.
- A slide show can be upgraded or changed easily.
- More people can get involved.
- Each picture has maximum impact.

However, if you have the money and the equipment or both, film is also an exciting adventure. We deal with that in the following chapter.

CHAPTER NINE

Film: Some Possibilities

The chair does not say "Director." Nobody is shouting "Quiet on the set!" and you won't recognize any of the heavies.

But the cameraoperator's face has a serious expression. He or she studies the roughly drawn illustration on the storyboard somebody has brought. "Is this the way you want it? Are you sure?"

"What's wrong?"

There is an elaborate consultation in the center of the yard. Some small children drift in, watch for a moment, and then one says, "Hey, can we be in the movie?"

This is an important project for a church with 150 members in which a group of young film-makers are earnestly trying to prepare for fellow Christians a film about themselves that "makes sense," as the director explains: "We have so many visitors who ask to know something about the church. Bits and pieces—that's what they get. It depends on the people they talk to. We want to give them the church as it is in every aspect of its life. We're using people of all ages in the film. A lot of people are excited about it, even those who aren't members. "You know," the director said, looking up, with eyes shining. "I think we've really got something here."

Many churches would agree with the young director who is helping bring to reality a project that could be the answer to the big question that plagues them all: How do we tell people about the church? How do we express our feelings about who we are?

"We'd like to do film but we don't have the equipment or the people. Sure, I think such a project would turn on a lot of people, really do the church a great deal of good but we just don't have, . . ." a minis-ter of a suburban church laments. "If I suggested a film, people would be upset. I can hear them saying 'this is the church, not Hollywood! What business does the church have in film-making?' "

Film-making, as an art medium, is as much the province of the church today as sculpture, painting, wood carving, and tapestry weaving were during the heyday of ecclesiastical arts in Europe. In addition, it is one of the most powerful communications media of this century, one which can distribute the Gospel message as easily as it can transmit scenes of violence and pornography.

Film is involving because the process of making a movie is universally exciting, because those on both sides of the camera are touched by the activity, because numbers of people have in some way to be committed to a project which makes obvious creative demands. Because film can be widely shared and the viewers are immediately reactive, a sense of community within the audience is naturally stimulated.

Film can assemble and recreate segments of the human drama while making a powerful and believable statement about it that makes the medium one of the most advantageous available for the Christian church in its task of presenting its vision about humankind.

How do you get started in film? It could begin when somebody says "Let's do one." or "Why couldn't we?" or "Wouldn't it be great?"

The initiators might be junior- or senior-high young people who have been exposed to film-making in high school. They are at ease with equipment. They know the possibilities because they have already done something in the field. Or the decision for film might come from some thoughtful middle-aged business execu-

Sixteen mm projectors can be borrowed or rented.

tives who have seen company training or sales films. "It gave me a very personal feeling about our company. Those of us who saw the film felt we were for the first time really able to know the organization of which we were a part." A middle-management person in business has been impressed with his first experience with film. He or she will be one of those who are enthusiastically supportive of such a project for the church. Interest and cooperation might come from anywhere, often from unexpected quarters.

Once decided on a film-making project, there immediately arises a bewildering set of choices. There is

16mm and, because many schools and some churches have 16mm projectors with which to show commercial films purchased or rented from distributing companies, that will be the most immediately familiar vehicle to a good many people. It is also the most expensive in terms of equipment and processing. Others will know 8mm, popular a decade ago, now largely superceded by what is called in the trade "super-8." Super-8 is popular and relatively inexpensive. It has been standardized with a variety of projecting equipment, most of it easily portable. Its capability is continually being expanded as manufacturers offer new refinements annually. The obsolescence of super-8 does not seem to be upon us at this time, so churches can invest with some confidence in the basic equipment necessary to do a creditable job.

A check with your talent bank which you, hopefully, have organized, will probably show a surprising number of super-8 cameras and projectors currently owned by church members. Some of these will be the property of people who know and understand them and are willing to teach others. Some are probably owned by people who bought them for their trip around the world, showed the film once or twice, and then forgot the whole thing. They might be willing to loan or to sell reasonably.

Asking someone to lend equipment to a group is a tricky procedure; a positive response would have to be one of love and faith. The dangers can be somewhat lessened if you are well organized in your borrowing and use procedures, and if you have made certain that equipment used by the church is adequately insured. One way to make lending more palatable is for the church to have a fund for repair and maintenance so that any minor damage can be handled without resorting to a claim against an insurance policy. A damage deposit can be asked of any one in the church using the equipment, even if it is a Church School class or a young people's group. They can be asked to post $50 deposit against the return of the equipment in good condition. Keeping a list of names of local service people in the equipment bank file is also a help. It might be a wise policy for the church to borrow only that equipment which can readily be serviced in its particular area. Some research into the servicing situation would be helpful at the very beginning of the film project.

The church may want to buy one basic super-8 package: camera, projector, and screen. Chances are it will be used well in comparison to the amount that will be spent. Some dealers give discounts to churches or church schools, a possibility that should be investigated. The several groups within the church that will be using the equipment might come forward with contributions to the fund.

Here some creative fund-raising projects might not only bring in the money required to buy the equipment but might also be a good way to get numbers of people excited about film-making. The more time the individual has invested in every aspect of the venture, the more interest he will take in it and the more inclined he will be to share that interest with others in the congregation. What projects? A "work" auction with people offering various services to church members for a price; a car, truck, and bus wash; a talent night with a panel of judges including some prizes;

acts from within the church and community; a ticket sale; an arts, crafts, or antiques fair with different groups participating on a percentage or fee basis. The cost of the booth goes into the equipment fund; all proceeds made from the sales go to the organization. This is easy to do and does not require much work of the sponsoring group other than an investment in time and some advance publicity. If enough money is realized, the original goal could be extended to include an editing package—film editor, splicer, as well as the cost of film and processing. Granted these are minor costs when compared with the equipment, but the less financially encumbered you are from the beginning, the more attention you can bestow on the job of making the film. Don't overlook the possibility of borrowing editors and splicers, several of each if possible, to make editing the film a project of as large a number of your creative group as possible.

There will still be people holding back, with substantial objections, from a film-making project. They will wonder if color slides won't do the same job a whole lot cheaper? Or if film will not be too complicated, involving too many people so as to take substantial numbers away from the other teaching avenues.

Admittedly, slides have their place and can do an excellent job in many ways. (See chapter eight). For many churches slides may be as far as they wish to go in visual communication. But film is a captivating medium that could inspire a ho-hum group of people to come alive. It invites broad participation—and therein lies its main value. It should not be considered an "instead of" way of learning the Gospel. As an involving medium it will tend to give people working in it a sense of community and will imbue with excitement many ideas and procedures that before seemed to be little more than routine. The criticism that only the young are interested in film is incorrect, as residences for senior citizens will testify all across the country where film-making has proved to be one of the most engaging and helpful activities for people of advanced years.

With equipment in hand or readily available, the church then needs to take its first step toward realization of the project.

The basic questions must be asked at the first planning session. Those who participate in this session may be representatives of all organizations in the church, anyone wishing to participate by open invitation, members of the communications committee, or any combination thereof. If the first film is to be done by a single department or group, it might still be wise to have some communications people aboard, at least at this stage.

The planners will be looking at such questions as:
1. What is the purpose of the film?
2. Why is film the better choice of media for doing the job we want to do?
3. What do we have in terms of equipment and people?
4. Do we want interaction between groups or do we want to keep shooting within a single group?
5. Will there be a deadline or some time limitation?
6. How much will production cost?
7. When and how often will the film be used?
8. Will this project have any effect on the whole church? What would we like that effect to be?

When the basic planning and some early work on the nature of the film has been done, it's time to spread the enthusiasm around. Film companies have their advance teams who go abroad and stimulate interest through a wide variety of stunts and gimmicks. Why not have an advance of your own? Put up posters on the church bulletin boards or stick them to the walls. Let people know that a film is coming. Let the congregation know what the needs of the film-makers might be, whether it's costumes, props, extras, or just a little technical assistance. Make this project belong in some way to everybody. You can run "teaser notes" in the church newsletter, include it in the announcements at services. Everybody should be aware of what is going on in their church. A spontaneous reaching out will result in fellowship as well as response to a specific request.

You will want to be creative, not just about doing the film itself but in the ways you go about preparing for it. We have already mentioned fund-raising projects for acquiring the necessary money. Now how do you get other necessities—apart from equipment—such as props, costumes, set? Why not have a great prop and costume hunt with some carnival touches? Get out lists of what you need. Have a day to go around and gather it, with all the gatherers in costume. Make a contest or fun outing of it for people of all ages. It's a good way to make contact with some of those people in the church who have been inactive. It's a good way to let others know that your church is enthusiastic and lively and that people enjoy being a part of its life. Get people on your bandwagon with a high-spirited invitation!

However, while everybody can be involved in some measure, there must be key people appointed (or maybe they will volunteer) to head up the major phases of the project. There should be a director or production chief, an equipment manager, and a script editor. The director might want an assistant or two to consult with him or her on various matters and to serve when the director cannot be present.

How many photographers will the film require? That, of course, depends on the length of film, the number of locations, the time schedule, and the complexity of the action. You can probably get along with just one camera person, but at the same time two or more will expand your capability and help pave the way for future film endeavors, some of which may be more ambitious than the first one. You can always use two people shooting a scene—one for background and establishing scenes, and another for shooting the action. Each cameraperson will need a script or set of instructions as to what to shoot. If each camera has a number, the director can relay instructions efficiently. Everybody involved will need a time schedule indicating where he or she is to be at what time so the work can progress with a minimum of delay.

APPROACHES TO FILM-MAKING

Early on you will probably be asking the question: What kind of film will we do? Will we present it as a drama, as an art form involving music, dance, perhaps pantomime? Will it be a communications film, a straightforward documentary, an accurate reflection of who we are and what we do?

The former will probably necessitate a script, characters, costumes, setting, special lighting, boom mikes, and some dedicated crew members. In another approach, the film-makers will take events as they come, recording them and finally editing them so that there is continuity and purpose. Producing this kind of film will require less formal preparation and equipment. The former may be a more complex and deeply involving project, requiring a great deal of time and thought.

Deciding which one of these you will want to do—or perhaps a combination of approaches—will probably be the first major decision to be made by the committee.

In the following pages we will go into some detail on the several approaches to film-making so that the film committee will know what it faces.

The Drama:

This could be a complex project, but even so a small church group could attempt a simplified version. It will probably involve script, characters, a set. You might be able to use a high school or community college studio in off time for a small rental fee. This would solve the problems of special lighting, boom microphones, special effects equipment. Alternatively, it could be shot entirely outdoors using natural light. You can purchase rights for limited production of an original play script which may be set up for film or which you can adapt. You can write your own, in which case the script would have to be in a form that could easily be followed, with the action detailed throughout. When your group first begins to talk over—brainstorm—a script idea, you will visualize the main action, the interaction between characters, and whatever purpose you hope to work within. Break the script down into short sequences to keep the structure tight and to give a manageable shooting schedule. Your script will have dialogue, setting description, action, camera instructions.

You might think of your script as a layout for a comic book, progressing from one point to another in frames of action, each with a readily visible change in relationship, angle, focus. It might be interesting and helpful to draw out your movie on a chart, much as you would develop the actions for a comic strip.

A script contest might be an opportunity to get the whole church involved and to give a blessing to the creative process. The "script" you are looking for might just be a one-page story idea which the script editor and his committee could develop. Or the church might want to use a drama created by a student in a local high school or community college. This sets up a useful link between church and community and would help generate interest in both the process and the finished project. If your film is well done and has been well received in your church, you might consider using it to pay back expenses by having a number of screenings for the community. A donation for the privilege of seeing the film would be nominal, but it would be helpful in trimming the cost of the project. You may even make enough to get ahead for expenses of the next film. You may want to go to other churches for help—both financial and personal. Strong ecumenical ties can develop through film-making. You might eventually have not only a mix of people in your own church but people from several denominations involved.

Some ideas for simple dramas: the difficulty of getting ages to mix—a situation in which some people who are elderly and some who are quite young learn to understand and appreciate each other; the aloneness of many people—two or three things happening to people who belong to the same church but who don't know each other; how the church deals with death, divorce, alienation, materialism, selfishness. There are countless dramas all around that can provide material for film-making. You can update a Bible story, write a modern parable, do the story of how the church changed the life of some one individual, dramatize a day in the life of a clergyman (few people appreciate the many demands on a minister's time).

If the drama is to be simple, you could probably construct or put together a set, shoot your film in natural light, use a script such as the dramatization of a Bible story in modern idiom, improvise "on the set," capture spontaneous action. This is a good first step into the adventure of film-making. It provides opportunity for direction and taking direction, handling camera, visualizing lines, tying in words and sound with action, and finally, editing and criticizing. There is the whole bowl of porridge, and you can add any additional ingredients you care to at any point along the way.

A film festival, of which there are a number—national, regional, and local—might move you to the point of decision making: you might send some of your enthusiasts out to view one or two of these to see what the possibilities are. Some film festivals are sponsored by high schools—particularly private and parochial institutions, where film-making seems to be more seriously ensconced—community colleges, museums, and schools of film-making and the arts. If there is no festival available, you might consider working with other established entities to sponsor one. All you need are rules, prizes, judges, and a place for screening. This kind of project could activate an entire community.

Plug into information sources that might tell you about film workshops or short courses in your area. Community colleges often offer noncredit film classes as enrichment courses off campus. Check with the colleges and universities in your area. Ask at major suppliers of film-making equipment. There is a possibility they may have mini courses or workshops from time to time. Such activities stimulate interest and sell cameras, so if there isn't one available, suggest its value both to your group and to the store. Offer to send interested people to such an event.

The Documentary:

You want to do a film but definitely not a drama. You want simplicity, authenticity, something that's historical, that faithfully reflects the life of the church. A documentary may be your choice. Most footage of a documentary should be factual, shot "live," though some can be simulated. You might shoot an event one year for presentation the next. You don't need an actual script, but you do need a shooting outline in order to make the most of the action and to develop a narrative feeling. As the event unfolds, the film record is made. Editing is an essential part of a documentary; initially, the film will be too loose and decentralized. It will need to have some continuity built into it. If the event or events are not sufficiently compelling, it might be that you would want to adopt a viewpoint and shoot from that. Shooting from a viewpoint means shooting from a personal idea of what the material's purpose is. It could mean the film is made through the eyes of someone in particular. A group of teens decided to shoot their documentary of church events through the eyes of a friendly dog. The idea sprouted from an unexpected visit one warm summer Sunday of a dog into the morning service. You might want to do a documentary on drug use in your community from the viewpoint of law enforcement, parents, medical profession, the user himself, or a mixture of these if you segment the film with sufficient clarity. Switching viewpoints without a clear understanding of why, or without transition, produces an aimless patchwork. It has to be done carefully. But the viewpoint question should be asked early on in the planning stage: "What point of view?" is as important as "What is the purpose of this film?"

Promotional Film:

Would this be appropriate for the church? Should the church promote, publicize, advertise itself as if it were a commercial product? No! Loud and clear. But being professional in any of these fields, utilizing the fruits of modern technology to share the Gospel message, is not blasphemy. The church gathers and scatters—the scattering can involve any one or all of these activities. A promotional film would do nothing more than tell a strong story from the viewpoint of the church and for the specific purpose of informing and generating interest in the activities of the church. And even though it records program in detail—from church school, church socials, men's club, women's association, prayer groups, youth organization—it still must make as its central point that what the church is all about is Jesus Christ. Promotional? So be it. Make a strong case for what is good. Why not? Through the medium of film we tell people who we are, what the Christian church is all about, why it is a good family to be part of. You might want to do this from the viewpoint of different members of the church, letting them speak over or in conjunction with the particular area of interest they represent. Or you may want to let the camera wander unselectively through the Christian week as it is celebrated in the church. Narration, which is a unifying factor as well as the means of keeping this film on the track, should be compelling, very direct, and professional. Music and other sound should be considered. If you have a sound camera, or cameras, you might ramble through and let people talk, spontaneously. "Hey, what do you like about

church . . . this church?" "Why do you turn up here Sunday after Sunday?" "What's so great about worshiping with others?" With lead questions developed in advance, and armed with little more, you can plunge directly into the life of the church for your promotional film.

Communication Film:

This has both promotional and documentary elements, though it may not "sell" as much as the one nor "relate" as much as the other. It may be more specific, expressive of some small story the church has to tell: How we work with young people. Our senior citizen's program. Some good and bad things about our church. What we need. Where we think we are going, and why we want to tell you about it. How our board (elders, vestry, etc.) operates. Those are the kinds of things that may need to be communicated. The communication film needs a script or at least a shooting plan, and a strong purpose. It needs narration. A brief interview, perhaps more than one, would work well here. This kind of approach could go beyond the church into the community: What is a big need in our town? How are other churches like (or unlike) ours? How does our town feel about minority housing, law enforcement, etc.? This would lead into photo journalism—telling a news- or issue-centered story with film. Brief interviews and close-up film— How do you feel about so and so?—make for strong, poignant emphasis.

Artistic or Symbolic Film:

Probably you have seen the abstract film-maker's art on public broadcasting: designs, distortions, macro focusing, diffusion, rapid cuts, dissolves, superimpositions. The effect can be bewildering as well as highly stimulating and fanciful. Abstract or impressionist film calls for unique ways of seeing ordinary things. It often involves playing with light as with a paintbrush and becoming highly involved with textures, shapes, and distance relationships. A film of this type would be an appropriate church school project for one age or all ages. You will want to consider narration, or a sound track consisting of music, sounds, mixtures of words, music and sound together. Poetry. A prayer. Wind bending trees, a leaf falling slowly, feathers drifting, a spider web being torn. Music will heighten the symbolism. The symbols may be used to dramatize a well-loved hymn. Or a prayer. Things could be filmed which seem to express human characteristics.

A junior high church school class decided to do their film on the Lord's Prayer. They wanted to symbolize the familiar words. That's all they knew in the beginning. But the question loomed: how to do it? Bread became the focal point. They filmed bread, and then more bread. Children throwing crusts to ducks on a pond, half a sandwich in a gutter, people eating sandwiches, buttering bread, bread coming out of the oven. They filmed the modern version of "bread"—money—and gradually went back into the opening portrayal of bread bits floating on the pond. They did temptation in terms of bread, trespasses in terms of bread. This film won an award in a local contest and eventually was much in demand for showings at churches. The young film-makers became part of a program which included the film and a workshop in which they talked about film-making and offered help to others considering it. As a result of this seed effort, a number of film groups were spawned and some good work developed. The workshop concept expanded and the interest continued at a high level.

Film Integrated with Live Action:

This could be done with any of the approaches heretofore considered. But particular mechanics for this kind of project might be a Bible story acted out over a film of church events. Film can be projected on a wall with action taking place in front of it. Film can be used to link actions. Or it can bridge the gap between then and now by shifting the attention of the audience from the live to the screen and back. It can be heightened and organized with narration or dramatic music bridges. This kind of film requires skillful handling of both staging and lighting.

There, briefly, are some possibilities. The broad generalizations here expressed are intended only to give some direction. There are many other versions of film, and the more you read about it the more aware you will become of the versatility and usefulness of the medium.

MECHANICS:

From content we go to mechanics. How to do it. For this you will need help either from experts resident in church or community, a representative from a film club or camera store, books and pamphlets—of which there is an inexhaustible supply. Don't start with heavy literature. Try some of Kodak's *Idea Book Series,* such as *Better Movies in Minutes* or *Home Movies Made Easy.*

Here's a brief idea of the content of a typical how-to-do-it: Special Events. Day-to-day Activities. Holidays. It goes on into film choices, types of cameras, loading, focusing, adjusting aperture, special lenses, lighting, sound, editing, splicing, titling.

A good source of information is the booklet that came with the camera you will use. You should know it well. You should know what the camera's capabilities are, how to adjust focus and light requirements, how to read the meter, how to set the film speed index, how to load, adjust lenses, change speed. Since there are so many different cameras on the market, each one a little bit different from the rest, it would be well to become thoroughly familiar with your particular manufacturer's handbook.

The camera you are using may have automatic exposure control. That's good—it's all done *for* you. It may have a low light indicator that tells you if the light is too low for your camera's capability. If you are required to set the lens opening, read the exposure guide on the camera. A typical one on a simpler camera may show sun, sun with clouds, cloudy, very cloudy, partial shade-partial sun. Opposite each of the pictograms will be the proper F-stop (lens opening). Set your F-stop to correspond with conditions. If yours has a fixed focus lens, everything will be in focus from a specified number of feet (probably four) on. You may have a range finder that, when the pieces of the split image are superimposed, puts you in focus.

If a filter is required, be sure you know where the filter switch is on your camera. Most cameras today have built-in filtration. You should know in advance the capability of your film. For example, Type G Ektachrome is all right for use indoors or outdoors without filter, but Kodachrome 40 Type A requires a filter for use in daylight though none is required if you are using movie lights indoors. Many of the new films are sufficiently fast that you can shoot in relatively low light situations without movie lights.

If your camera has a battery-operated film transport system, all you have to do is push the button and the film progresses. Older cameras should be rewound after each shooting. Batteries should be checked periodically. Read and understand the built-in battery check.

Zooming

A recent addition to movie cameras, the zoom extends capability. Too frequently zoom becomes a fascination or a play toy. Don't overzoom. The effect is like eating a heavy meal and descending in a fast elevator. The big advantage in a zoom is that before you start shooting you can frame the picture in exactly the way you want it—medium, close, or distant. Focus is tricky. Be sure, particularly when in telephoto, to be sharp. You don't

It is possible to photograph TV. Make sure there are no reflections. Use a tripod.

have as much depth of field in this mode. Some zooms focus poorly at close and telephoto range but do all right in between. Some lose sharpness at the middle range. Some are consistently sharp over the whole focal length range. Study and ask questions about the focusing capability of the camera you will be using. Read comparisons of lenses or ask your camera store salesman.

Many cameras have both manual and power zoom. The latter is indicated by a switch that says "tele" and "wideangle." Pushing the one you want will zoom you into either range. If the camera has a macro set lever, you can get dramatic close-ups, excellent for nature photography and for titles.

To make zoom shots interesting, frame objects with objects such as trees, a fence, a wall. The camera, zooming, will tend to draw the audience into the picture. Or shoot from an angle that includes a strong foreground such as a road or an expanse of open field.

As the zoom moves through its ranges, it will have a tendency to draw in the foreground in such a way that it will seem to be moving right under the audience's feet.

The zoom can be used to lead the audience in to a scene. You might begin with a tight close-up, then zoom back to reveal more and more of the scene. Also you can do jump cutting—zoom with camera on a tripod, zoom for a second, stop, zoom again, stop and zoom again until you reach the end of the zoom, then cut the shot. This gives a feeling of time passing. You could visualize this by zooming on a clock and resetting the hands at each zoom. This technique should not be used more than once in a film because it readily loses its value.

Variety is the spice of a good film. Right or wrong? Right. Vary distance and viewpoint. If you are shooting a parade, take the parade approaching, a shot of the sun glinting off a tuba, kids watching close-up, a child on his father's shoulders, an old lady holding her purse and staring intently, a small boy trying to see, people wiping sweat off their faces, a child staring, dripping ice cream, the parade, the reaction, back to the parade, and maybe when it's all over, the street—the silent litter, the empty reviewing stand, a dog sniffing in the rubbish. Vary scene length. At the normal camera speed of 18 fps (frames per second), it takes the same amount of time to show the sequence as to film it. You may need just a second or two for an established shot, longer for close-ups or action. Extreme close-ups are possible with macro focusing lenses or with a series of close-up attachments that you can buy for just a few dollars.

Here is the place to say that you need a good solid tripod and a cable release. There are times when you can't have any equipment motion at all. For example, when you are shooting at 24 fps. In this case, tiny movements are magnified on the screen. This will give you a fine slow motion effect that helps add detail, but if your camera is jiggling or your hand-activated shutter is nervous, you'll have a scene that looks as if it's going through a butter churn. Though you will do most shooting at 18 fps, you will want to switch to 12 fps to speed up someone approaching the camera, fast cars, etc. You also get a half stop more with 12 fps which helps in dim light. Shooting at 24 fps slows down action so you can see detail. You can make a dancer float through the air, an athlete will reveal an inner feeling of surprise as he misses a pass. These heroic moments will have more meaning in a slower mode.

When in an extremely dimly lighted situation, you can shoot at 9 fps. This gives you twice as much exposure as normally and speeds up the action so that you get a comedy effect. Unless you want this special effect, use just a slightly slower than normal camera speed for stationary or slow moving objects shot in normal light.

With fast films, and the new design of many movie cameras that allows all light from a subject to reach the film, you can get by in a good many situations without extra lighting. Light weight, easy-to-carry movie lights especially designed for specific cameras are widely available and produce as much light as the old cumbersome movie light bars. If your camera has automatic exposure control, you need do no more than aim and film, just as you would to make daylight movies. You're OK as long as you are within the distance range capability of the light.

The automatic electric eye of many advanced design cameras today takes care of exposure in most situations, except that if you have a strong backlight or other light source to contend with, you will have to take close-up readings off the skin of your subject to avoid silhouette. You will then have to put the camera on manual and set the exposure according to your meter reading. When light is very low, stick to strong close-ups. Note: Some newer models have a built-in back lighting switch to meter the subject in situations of a strong light source.

Panning

We've talked about zooming. Another area into which you will want to wander is panning. Take note of these ground rules and then do some experimenting. Go from the most important part of the scene to the least important. Film several seconds of the main part of the scene without moving the camera, then move the camera slowly and steadily to encompass the remainder of the scene. End by holding on the last view for a few seconds. To pan action, move in the direction of the action, keeping focused on the subject of the action. The rest of the subjects will be blurred. Hold the camera firmly and pivot at the hips. Shoot at 12 fps so they'll look as fast as they are.

Your camera may have single frame capability (SFC) for animation or shooting stills such as posters, paintings, slides, and maps.

With SFC you can produce all kinds of unusual effects. To make a puppet's arm move, for example, you will decide that a single movement should take one second on the screen so you shoot the movement in 18 steps. Each time you move the arm slightly you shoot one frame. When you project the footage, the arm appears to be moving. It's the same with cartoons. You make separate drawings, each showing a different stage of the action, and each drawing is filmed in sequence. With SFC you can shoot clay figures, collages, chairs falling over by themselves, pots rising off the stove.

You can work out your entire film in terms of footage using the basic 18 fps and deciding how long you want each sequence to last. If the sequence takes 18 seconds, for example, you will need 180 frames.

You may want to do time lapses—the opening of a flower, the fading glory of a sunset. Divide 190 into one hour and you get 3,600 seconds (the total time that will elapse). Shoot one frame every 20 seconds. Shooting a sunset, put your lens on infinity, the camera on a tripod, use a cable release, start with 15 or 18 single frames, then shoot one frame every 20 seconds. Your automatic aperture control will adjust for the changing light as the sun sinks (or you may have to read the meter and adjust if it isn't automatic). For interesting effects you can add one or more filters during the filming.

You can even make movies without a camera! Using a reel of unexposed film and a sharp pointed instrument like the end of a compass needle scratch designs into the film on the emulsion side and then project it. Or you can soak it in hypo or chlorine bleach to get rid of the emulsion, and then paint designs on it with a small camel's hair brush or felt tip pens. Sometimes used news film is obtainable from a TV station. This is easier to do using 16mm film but you need a 16mm projector. You can do it with super 8 but the frame size is quite small. You might manage by doing it under a magnifying glass.

Prices

In a recent photography magazine we read through prices. It was usually impossible to tell what kind of package you were getting for the price noted. You would need to get the model number of the equipment, ask to see it at a local camera store or consult one of the equipment annuals put out by the major photography magazines. Otherwise, it's hard to know what you're getting. Example:

Camera A: Available light, f 1.2 Zoom 4-1 macro focusing, backlight adjustment, split image range finder, built-in fade in-fade out, built-in intervalometer for time lapse photography, single frame adjustable eyepiece, with handgrip: $169.95

Camera B: Low light, 2x power zoom, electric eye, auto metering, footage counter, fl.8 lens: $49.95

Camera C: Zoom 8-64mm f 1.8 power zoom 3 speeds including slow motion, TTL meter, through the lens focusing and viewing, battery tester: $163.95

Best way may be to make a list of those qualities you think you really need and then try to get them for the least amount of money: zoom, automatic metering, footage counter, fast lens (1.8), hand grip, good range of speeds (fps). Focusing throughout the zoom range is important so it should be checked carefully before buying. But probably at this time a good adequate motion picture camera without sound can be had for under $200.00. With sound, under $300.00. Not a bad investment for a church to make.

Sound

We haven't said much about sound before this because it is not a necessity. You can always record sound and have it striped onto your film by one of the companies that offers such service. Cost is around 2¢ a foot. Problem here may be exact sync. The sound/movie camera offers a number of sophistications

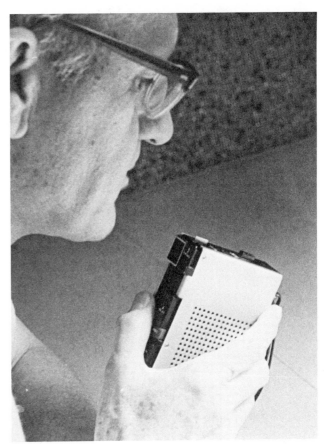

The condenser mike.

including sound that runs at 24 fps rather than being limited to 18 fps, manual level adjustment (instead of automatic gain control), automatic fade; some even combined with picture fade for one touch operation. Sound cameras—and there's a wide tribe of them—are more compact than ever, so you don't sacrifice ease of handling. There are highly directional condenser mikes, some on booms that slide onto the body of the camera or that project out above the lens. Others have conventional directional mikes that jack into the camera's recorder.

Choices

Some ground rules: Have the microphone as close as possible to the source of the sound so that is the dominant sound and will be picked up by the automatic gain control (unless yours has manual level adjustment) in the camera amplifier. Best results are achieved by the mike's being one to five feet from the sound source. Be sure it's not in the picture area!

The closer your mike is to the sound source, the less the possibility of having garbled sound and overwhelming camera noise. Be sure to keep the mike at

New equipment hits the market every month or so.
Here is a film/tape splicing device.

least several feet from the camera to reduce mechanical distortion. This is especially necessary when using an omnidirectional microphone, the kind on most cameras.

If the speaker is talking and you don't want the mike in the picture, frame him in very close. Be sure that when the speaker is holding the mike he does not jiggle it, hit it against anything, or move the cord sharply. All of these things come out on your soundtrack as unlovely, sometimes startling, noises.

A good way to see if your sound is pure and clear is to use the earphone supplied with your camera to premonitor the sound so that you can place the mike for best results. Be sure to check the batteries, prefera-

bly after every six cartridges of film is shot, or you may be going to a lot of trouble for nothing.

Omnidirectional mikes are fine for a quiet studio situation, but for most movie-making a cardioid or unidirectional microphone is recommended. This is offered as an accessory by most camera manufacturers. Some come on a boom that shoes onto the camera. When you purchase one be sure it matches the camera and be sure your camera has the capacity to accept the add-on.

Some quick don'ts for sound production: 1. Don't place the mike on a hard surface. Provide padding under it. 2. Don't record in rooms with large hard surfaces which will bounce the sound. 3. Don't record within hard surfaces outdoors. Shoot out in the open or where there are bushes and trees. 4. Don't shoot when the wind is very high. You can cover the mike with a handkerchief to cut out wind noise except where it is exceedingly loud.

Editing and Splicing

This can be a problem in the case of a sound film. There may be an 18-frame separation between picture and sound on film. You can wind up with unrelated sound at the beginning and end of your film, so it is best not to record sound for one or two seconds at the beginning and end of each scene. Note: Some newer models have an auto sound kick which eliminates sound lag at the beginning. When using splicing tape you will have to tip it slightly so it doesn't cover the sound stripe. You will want to splice your film so that it will all go on one 200- or 400-foot reel for showing (about 15–30 minutes of viewing time all told). A good accessory we've seen offered is an editing tray which has 24 wells in it to keep 24 separate scenes or short cuts in proper order. Each segment is coded with a piece of white tape on which is marked a shot number. A short description of the show is then written on three-by-five index cards and keyed with the same number as that on the tape. When you are ready to put the film in order, juggle the cards into the sequence you want and then put the film in the same order. Though this is offered by some film suppliers at a cost of less than $10 it would be entirely possible to devise one of your own, perhaps using egg boxes or cardboard separators. You can buy a "film editor" consisting of film rewinds and viewer that lets you view, find, cut, and splice. Or you can use just a splicer and splice tape using a reel on your projector to hold and wind film while splicing. Many of the newer projectors have small previewing screens that help immeasurably in editing film.

Projectors

A wide range of projectors is available from $60 to over $400: these are sound, silent, dual 8, super 8. Newer ones are called movie decks and look a lot like carrousel slide projectors. Features you should check: ease of loading, ease of carrying and handling, lens quality, lamp brightness (50 vs. 80 watt), fast forward, instant rerun, and projection speed options.

Another dimension to super 8 enables the film to be

Projectors of new design are easier to handle, less complicated to use.

transferred to video tape, from whence it can be put on a video tape deck and played through a home set or monitor. There is at this writing a unit made by Kodak called a Supermatic Film Videoplayer costing somewhere around $1,000, which displays super 8 film on any TV screen, silent or with striped sound. This can be wired into multiple sets for group showings. It features 18 or 24 fps playing speeds. This might be a little more involved than a church would want to become but all new technology should be looked at when any substantial investment in communications hardware is to be made.

"Our Church Picnic": A Shooting Script

Audio	Film
Sprightly Music	Little girl holds up a poster that says: Our Church Picnic, St. John's Methodist Church, July 19, 1976. She looks at it, turns it upside down, looks at it again, turns it right side up. The second time it's another poster saying: Cast: the congregation. Directors: John Murray and Cathy Weingart. A third poster gives other credits. Pull back to show child standing with poster as other children join her. They throw a ball to her, she drops the
Narration Begins	
This is the story of our church picnic. To begin with, we want to say why we have such a thing as a church picnic year after year.	
We do it for fun, for fellowship, and for a relaxing time of family gathering because we feel it is important to remember that the church is a family and that everyone of us is important.	

poster, catches the ball. They begin to play.

Close-up of people putting on name tags, and medium shot of minister greeting people. Medium shots of people arriving, getting out of cars with lawn chairs. Close-up of man cooking hot dogs, his face full of smoke. Medium shots of families. Close-up of old man, child on his lap. Child eats hot dog, old man wipes mustard off child's face.

During the course of the film other shots are brought in: a bunch of balloons floating toward the sky, flowers along the walkway, somebody picking up paper cups, close-up of ice cubes floating in a bowl of punch, paper cups blowing off a table. Races far off with people watching in background. Close-ups of winners straining at the finish.

The sound in a film like this is not critical because the narration does not specifically tie into the action. This is a simple kind of film to make but at the same time it can be a challenging creative exercise, a good cornerstone for your beginning Christian film-making community.

We have not covered every possibility, every sophistication available even for amateur film-makers, nor did we intend to do so. Our goal has been, rather, to explore briefly the potential for the church in film-making, how the project itself and its peripheral activities can involve the whole church in an adventure of communication. Film-making is richly creative, deeply personal, and at times a startlingly revelatory experience for all involved. We feel that it is important as a means of expressing not only what we do in the Christian church but who we are.

CHAPTER TEN

External Communication: "The Great Turkey Race"

"Why isn't our church in the newspapers more often? I see other church's news being mentioned all the time. In a small town like ours, it's important to be in the papers . . ."

If that is your story, the immediate course of action is to find out whether or not your church has sent any material to the local paper. From that point on, it may be necessary to do some research into just what is going on in communications in this church anyway.

Newspaper Releases

If there are people in your church who are sending in the news in a readable manner in accordance with deadlines, there is no reason why some of your church's news should not be getting into dailies and weeklies in your area. Of course, the better your material is, the more in conformity with newspaper style and format, the bigger dent you will make in the problem. At this point organizing a working group of communications people (see chapter one communications committee) would be a way to insure against future deficits of this kind.

We are going to consider in the first part of this chapter one event in the life of a local church and how it could be handled so as to produce the most satisfactory results in terms of volume and accuracy of coverage. The event is a church bazaar which, because it is to take place in the Thanksgiving season, has for its highlight a turkey race. There are also, of course, all the usual events such as barbecue, arts and crafts, a flea market. The church is a missionary minded church with 60% of its annual budget being spent for work

outside the congregation. The people of the church—which we will call St. Christopher's—are friendly, deeply involved in the life of the community. St. Christopher's hopes to derive from its bazaar the following:

1. Funds to continue its missionary work, particularly in India.
2. A broadening of fellowship with others in the community.
3. A way to attract new people in the area and to let them know of the existence of St. Christopher's.
4. An opportunity for those who enjoy expressing themselves creatively to share their work with others.
5. A form of service option in which people can give their time and effort (if not their money) to further the work of the church.

The communications committee of St. Christopher's has agreed to handle the task of communicating the event. There will be continuing relationships already established which have served well with local media. People involved in the bazaar will serve as resource people from whom the communicators can get their facts.

The five purposes of the bazaar will be enunciated in such a way that the whole church is aware of them. They will be integrated into information contained in news releases. Two tasks immediately confront the communications committee:

1. *Task One:* They must know the subject well, have the facts at hand, know the underlying philosophy of the event.

2. *Task Two:* They must be able to write and place news about the event in local media.

Task One is taken care of by conferring with the minister or pastor of the church and the principals of the event. A bit of history is consulted if the bazaar has been an annual event for some years. The communications committee and the bazaar chairpersons may have at least one session to brainstorm ideas for communicating the event. Part of the search will be for news angles which will make the bazaar even more interesting to the news media than it normally would be.

Task Two is achieved by following old-line principles of writing and presenting a news release.

1. At the top of the page place the name, address, and telephone number of the person presenting the release, in this case a member of the communications committee assigned to the task. Place this person's title or role (such as publicity or communications chairperson) adjacent to his or her name.

2. About 20 spaces down from the top of the page write the name of the publication to which the release is being sent, and below that the date on which you wish the story to be released. Both should be lined up flush left. A release date can be noted as IMMEDIATE. Or ANYTIME AFTER (DATE). Or ANYTIME BEFORE (DATE). Or it can be specific: RELEASE WEDNESDAY, JULY 14.

By leaving those 20 spaces you've given room for the editor to write in a headline or instructions to the printer. Be good enough thereafter to leave fairly wide right and left margins so that other editing marks can be written in if necessary.

Double space. Use a good typewriter ribbon. Use standard capitals and lower case form. *Never* write anything in the story IN ALL CAPITALS (like this). For style, look over the publications for which you are writing. Note what they capitalize and what they abbreviate, and follow that as far as is practical.

Leave at least ten spaces at the bottom of the page so the editor can write "MORE" if there is more, or "30" if that's as much as he will use. If you can get all of your story on one page, so much the better. You might save yourself the possibility of being edited.

Be simple throughout your story. Be concise. But don't be dull. If there is something unusual, exciting, interesting about your event, lead off with it. Pull out the highlights and let their glow shine over all your story. Be sparing of adjectives. A few will suggest themselves but you won't have to go looking for them. Use active words, adhering to basic principles of good writing. (See chapter three.)

Here is how the first newspaper release might read:

From: Joe Blow, Communications Director, St. Christopher's Any-Denom-
    inational Church, P.O. Box 3430, New Town, Mich. 33450 343-5264

OCT. 7, 19XX
TO: NEW TOWN GAZETTE
FOR IMMEDIATE RELEASE

A turkey race will be the feature attraction of the annual St.

Christopher's Non-Denominational Church's Thanksgiving Bazaar Oct.12-13

on the church grounds, 2216 Smith St. The race, which begins at 8:30 p.m.,

Friday will pit Uncle Tom Turkey, the number one racing gobbler from

Winnebago, Minn. against Big Wallis, pride of New Town. Sixteen other

turkeys from throughout the South and Southwest will also compete. Big

Wallis, owned and trained by Tom Wharton, an elder in St. Christopher's

Church, is said to be in top shape and a favorite to grab off the Silver

Turkey Challenge Cup which has been won by Uncle Tom for the past three

years. Sidney Brown, Farm Editor for Radio Station DRBE, will call the

race.

This is the fourth year for the bazaar, which was begun in 19XX

to expand community fellowship and to give creative church members a chance

to exhibit their works to the public. Items to be offered for sale during

this year's event include Christmas decorations, hand-made quilts, baked

goods, toys, and miscellaneous items collected into a giant flea market.

Foods, including barbecue chicken by the plate or beef by the pound, will

be sold. Bazaar hours are from 7:30 p.m. to 10 p.m.

All proceeds from the bazaar will go into the church's missionary

program through which the congregation supports two working clergymen in

Calcutta, India.

_____	Basic Facts
_ _ _ _ _ _	Possible Leads
================	Description

This gives both color and facts. If you think one or more of the papers might use a longer version, you might add some quotes about the race and the purpose of the bazaar, number of people expected to attend based on last year's attendance, more details about arts and craft items, names of chair people. These could all be put on the second page, giving the paper the option of using either the short (but very complete) form or of launching into the expanded version. There are several possibilities for leads in the above story. There are cold basic facts which if lifted out of the story would still give adequate information. There are some philosophical and descriptive comments that may or may not be used. A good basic exercise in recognizing the ingredients of a news story would be to try to pick out these three ingredients—basic facts, possible leads, description. We have underlined them in the story.

If you are including a photograph—perhaps one of the challenging turkey, its owner, and the radio announcer who will call the race—you would want to append to it an identification sheet giving the names of people (and turkey) left to right and some brief facts. The photo cutline should be able to stand alone as a news story in the event there is not room for both.

Here, a sample cutline

Big Wallis, center, declares himself to be ready to take on Uncle Tom Turkey and other challengers in Friday's Great Turkey Race at the St. Christopher's Any-Denomination Church Bazaar, 345 Smith Street. His owner, Tom Wharton, seems to agree, but Sidney Brown, KRBE Farm Editor and judge for the big race, isn't so sure. Tickets for the race, which highlights the church's two-day bazaar and barbecue are available at the church or may be bought at race time, 8:30 P.M., Friday. —Jim Brown Photo

It is a courtesy to include a photo credit line as shown. Paste cutline to the bottom of the print.

When the releases are typed and ready to mail, and the photo is at hand with its cutline, there remains the question of whether or not to send the same release to several papers. How about the same photo? If the papers to which you are sending are noncompetitive (weeklies serving several small towns), you might send the same photo and story (photo copied or otherwise duplicated), typing in the name of the publication on each. If the papers you are reaching have overlapping circulation and you don't have too many to contact, you might write a separate release with a new lead for each one. You can pull specifics out of the list of events to take place and play up different ones to give you a variety of lead possibilities. You can, for example, lead with the owner of the turkey, the radio announcer, the number of people expected to attend, some statistics on the race itself. The body of the story can be the same; only the lead need be different. If you are using quotes, you could quote different people in the several stories.

Here is a quick last-minute checklist to apply to your news presentation:

1. Is the form acceptable—typed double space with a good ribbon, room at top, bottom, and sides for editing?
2. Is your name and phone number at the top for contact?
3. Is the release date at the top?
4. Are all names spelled correctly? Is capitalization correct? Particularly, have you included *no* words in all capitals (a common horror)?
5. Do you have the basic facts?
6. Do you have a biography and picture of the principal in the story if it seems appropriate (new minister, out-of-town speaker, award winner, etc.)?
7. Is the story reasonably short (not over two pages)?
8. Does the date tie in with the tense used and the publication date of the paper or magazine? (Another common horror: a future tense story that obviously has not been sent in time to make a "future" edition of the publication.)
9. Have you listed only the names of the principals in the story rather than the dozens of people who have figured in the event? Newspapers do like names, but they don't like lengthy lists of names. Pare yours down to four or five people who serve in leading roles.

10. If there is an accompanying photo, have you attached an identification line indicating the people depicted left to right, giving their full names and titles?
11. Have you sent in a brief covering note requesting that the editor use the story if possible and thanking him in advance?

THE RADIO RELEASE

This is similar to the newspaper release except that as the form varies somewhat the writing will have to be more succinct.

Type on right half of the page, all caps. Use no more than 85 words for a 30-second spot and no more than 175 for a one-minute announcement. Leave the station free to pick the times in which the spot is to be used. It is perfectly all right, however, to suggest public service or community news slots or even to indicate a preferred time period (when you think most of your audience will be listening).

The Spot

Your name, title, address, and phone (as on newspaper release)
To: Name of Radio Station
Subject: 1 Min (or 30 Sec) Spot
Client: St. Christopher's Any-Denominational Church
Time: Any public service or community news availability (or specify time period)
Release: Begin Oct. 9 End Oct. 14, 8 P.M.

(Thirty Sec) THE TURKEYS ARE GOING TO TROT FRIDAY NIGHT AT 8:30 P.M. AT ST. CHRISTOPHER'S ANY-DENOMINATIONAL CHURCH, 326 SIXTH STREET, AS 18 FAST-RUNNING BIRDS COMPETE IN THE GREAT TURKEY RACE FOR THE SILVER CHALLENGE CUP. IT'S ALL PART OF THE FUN, FOOD, AND FELLOWSHIP OFFERED BY ST. CHRISTOPHER'S IN ITS ANNUAL TWO-DAY THANKSGIVING BAZAAR. DOORS OPEN AT 7:30 P.M., FRIDAY AND SATURDAY. EVERYONE'S INVITED. PROCEEDS SUPPORT THE CHURCH'S OVERSEAS MISSIONARY PROGRAM.

TELEVISION NEWS

This is similar to a radio release except that you should call the TV station first and determine what copy they can use, what materials in terms of copy and visuals they would prefer to have. They may want a slide, an example of a poster somebody has made, a photographic print. If they want such material, you could either set up a shot or you might have something left over from last year's bazaar that would do. With the slide they would probably use about 15 seconds worth of copy.

This is the form.

Name, Release info, etc. at the top (similar to Radio)
Public Service Spot

Video	Audio
Slide	NOW YOU CAN HELP SUPPORT MISSIONARY PROGRAMS IN INDIA. BRING THE WHOLE FAMILY THIS WEEKEND TO ST. CHRISTOPHER'S BIG THANKS-GIVING BAZAAR AND TURKEY RACE, ---- SMITH STREET. FRI-DAY AND SATURDAY 7:30 P.M. TO 10 P.M. PROCEEDS WILL BE USED TO BUY BIBLES FOR IN-DIAN SCHOOL CHILDREN.

Triple space. Send several copies.

Do not fail to inquire of all media if they would prefer an approach other than a straight news story. Or if they would like a follow-up. Offer to help get together a feature story, have someone come to the studio for an interview, participate in a station promotion. Offer photographs, complete stories, people and props for interviews or to set up same for their photographer. Say, "I'll be happy to get together whatever you'd like when and where you'd like it." Then be sure the people you contact will be there, and check back with the station to let them know the assignment is "on." Offer help in covering the event as well, setting up photos when requested, bringing people forth for interview, working with the media representatives on the site in whatever way they wish.

POST-EVENT COVERAGE

Is this important? Who cares, now that Uncle Tom Turkey has won (again) and the bazaar is over? But there is a whole new story here after the event ends. How much money was made? Who won the turkey race? How many people attended? Will there be a bazaar next year?

Every event has two stories—the one about its taking place and the one that tells what happened. Unfortunately many communications people get off the job at the point where it is only half done.

Sometimes it is hard to get a post-event story placed because of the great demand for space to be used by upcoming and current news. But many weeklies will be interested in who won the prize, what the speaker said, who was elected. If the church is entertaining a speaker of some note who is going to say things of interest to the general public, the communications committee would probably want to have the event covered by someone taking notes or making tapes or both. Often it is easy for one person to do both. Taking key notes while taping helps the writer, particularly if he or she has tied the notes into the referral spot on the tape by making a marginal notation giving the approximate place on the tape where the material is located (a counter is handy for this). In this way the story can be written without the necessity of running through the entire tape, and good quotes can be picked out to beef up the facts.

If you think your event would warrant photography—something you might discuss with the paper to which you plan to submit the material—you might offer to work with their photographer or provide one of your own. Be sure your cutlines are written and pasted to the photo before it is sent. Be sure you have the names of people accurately listed left to right.

Time is important in covering an event, even though the urgency may not be felt as it is in handling advance publicity. To keep the story out of the category of "yesterday's news," the writer should lead with a quote from the speaker regarding the future, the community, how policy will be carried out—anything that will lead the reader out of the event itself into the area of greatest general interest. Also the story and photo must be in the hands of the publication as soon as possible after the event. Strive to make the next deadline. Don't put it off for a week or two and then try to breathe life into it. This means the communications committee will be working twice under pressure, but they may find, as most newspaper reporters have, that they do their best work that way.

APPRECIATING THE MEDIA

After it is really all over—pre and post—you might want to contact the media people with whom you have worked and simply say "thanks." Your willingness to work with them, your enthusiasm for what you are doing, and your gratitude for what they have done will inspire them to give you continuing cooperation. Publicity for the next event will be that much easier to handle. You build trust and at the same time you learn *to* trust, expressing your confidence by not telling them how to write the story or what page of the paper to put it on. A simple thank you from you, or even several brief notes of thanks from people in your church, will insure good relations. A letter from the minister to the editor praising the reporter who worked with you, or one to the station manager praising the public service director—both are good ways to respond. If the story should not suit you or certain members of the church, don't complain about it unless the reporter has been guilty of some damaging inaccuracy. Vow to be more specific, more direct, next time. And refrain from threatening a working press person with "weight." "I know the managing editor," "I know the publisher." You'd be surprised how often such threats are used by people who should know better.

Some churches have taken their media appreciation a step further by celebrating a special media appreciation day in their community with reporters invited to a reception in their honor, at which time they are properly thanked for all they have done. It is helpful to invite representatives of the media to the church to speak from time to time. Many reporters, radio and TV newsmen and women are entertaining speakers, and often they will speak for you without a fee as a part of the medium's public relations program. You might ask media people to help educate your communications committee. Invite reporters to some of your more interesting events, not as reporters all the time but merely as guests. Send them gratis tickets. They may not care to come but they will undoubtedly be pleased that you made the friendly gesture.

A clergyman who was also formerly head of the department of promotion of a large protestant adjudicatory in the eastern part of the country sees the job of external communications as being largely a matter of the attitude of the communicator. He recalls how, when new on the job, he called on the editor of a large metropolitan daily whose religious news section had been going downhill badly. As he waited to see the religious news editor, a woman standing next to him vowed she had come on the same mission—to place some church copy. He glanced at her material. It was handwritten, almost illegible. "I couldn't read it and for that matter neither could she," he recalled. "The city editor complained that most of the material received from church contributors was that bad. I laid before him a neatly typed, double-spaced story about a church event in the city. He was delighted. From that point on he would use anything I wrote. We became friends. We lunched together on occasion. I never brought stuff to him with a demand that he use it, but I always expressed thanks when he did. I made a good many personal visits to him through the years, handing him copy rather than dropping it in the mail. I offered my services any time he needed specific information on something church-connected where I could help. I found other clergy amazed at how much material of mine was published. 'What's your secret?' I was frequently asked. No secret. Just a matter of being professional about copy, being available to offer services, being open and forthright, showing appreciation. You don't tell the editor of a paper what to do—you offer. It's a matter of attitude. The same goes for television. I believe strongly in the value of making personal contacts. I once brought my entire congregation down with me to the local TV studio. That was impressive. We in the church have a significant audience which we can influence to some extent. That's important to TV stations."

CHAPTER ELEVEN

Advertising: We Pay Our Way

Legitimate claims on the white space of a newspaper, or on air time of radio or TV, may be made with news events or features of general interest. But what about other possibilities for getting the word out? An advertising budget. Now the elders or board of deacons will throw up their hands in horror as will the head of finances. But it makes good sense to build a small advertising budget into every event the church sponsors for fund-raising purposes. This money can be used to buy notices in the local papers, some spots on radio, or even TV if the event is significant enough to warrant a sufficiently large budget. Maybe you would like signs, posters, or handbills. Something more professional than those turned out by the church school kindergartners, though those too have their place in communications.

When should advertising an event or the church itself be considered?

1. When you have not been getting the amount of space for legitimate news that you feel is needed and warranted because the papers cover too much territory and have too little editorial space.

2. When you feel the importance of the event warrants more than one communications thrust.

3. When you would like to run a phone number for direct response, or a coupon.

4. When you would like public exposure of your church's logo or picture, or would like to get some direct message to the public that would not be politic in a news story.

5. When you would like to know that you will be occupying so much space, and when you might want to say when your message will appear and on what part of the page.

6. When you want to get out an audience for a radio or television program of interest to your congregation.

7. When you want radio or TV announcements at a specified time of day so as to reach the widest audience.

PUTTING TOGETHER AN ADVERTISEMENT

In putting together an ad for print media it is always well to enlist the services of a professional in layout. This will cost you, but it will protect your investment and assure you of maximum effectiveness for your advertising message. A poorly laid out ad can easily be lost or overlooked on a busy page. If the message is not simple, direct, and strong, your money will have been virtually wasted.

Alternatively, many publications—including newspapers—have art departments with professional artists who can specify type; suggest a simple border; size a halftone; position elements in a prescribed area, preserving the criteria of readability, neatness, and balance. Ask for a prepublication proof if you decide to go this route.

If no artists reside on the church's doorstep or are within calling distance or are within your price range, it is possible that the art department of a local high school or junior college might come to your aid. You might help develop a budding talent. Be sure he or she knows the mechanical requirements of the medium you are to use.

Actually almost anyone can put together an acceptable ad by studying advertisements, taking note of principles of design they follow, utilizing those same basics. This should be resorted to if there is no way to contact an experienced artist.

A Photographic File

Any church considering running advertising on any regular basis would do well to put together a file of photographs of church-sponsored events, personnel, and buildings. These should be black-and-white glossy prints, identified by a strip of paper affixed to the bottom, pasted or taped to the back of the photo. Never write with pencil or ballpoint on the back of a photo. Prints should be 5-by-7 or 8-by-10 except in the case of portraits (mug shots) of personnel, in which case they can be 4-by-5 or even smaller. They should be subject-filed along with negatives so that a replacement print can be made when one is sent out. In the case of 35mm negatives, which are usually stored in strips of five or six, each negative should have a code number which is noted on the back of the print. It is well to have more than one print in the file for much-used subjects. Do not ask a newspaper to return your photos. Some will but most won't, and many consider it an imposition.

A Clip Art File

Another useful file to have for advertising, brochures, or mailing pieces of many kinds is one of clip art, consisting of black-and-white line drawings of various subjects, borders, and decorative accent material such as you see in newspapers or magazines. Be sure you are not clipping something bearing an artist's signature, such as a cartoon, or one which is obviously protected by copyright. There appears daily a wealth of line drawings and accent material suitable for use as clip art. Though not all of it will be useful for the church's particular needs, it should not be difficult to get together a good array of suitable material. Dark red, brown, or black will print black in a black-and-white ad. Blue or light green will "drop out," that is, not show. Clip things that will print, illustrations with strong, well-defined lines that can be traced onto a stencil or that will photograph well (for offset reproduction). All clippings should go into the communications art file. Also into that file might go fancy large or capital letters and perhaps some good strong type—even whole words or sentences you might want to use. There are art clipping services, some which offer illustrative material particularly for churches. You could investigate the cost of one of these if you plan to

do several direct mail pieces that would need continuity as well as variety of illustration. Many churches use clip art for their regular news bulletins—and often they seem to be subscribing to the same services, for a cross-section look at such bulletins in a single area tends to reveal a large number of similarities. That's not necessarily bad as most churches mail newsletters to members only, but there is still satisfaction to be gained in using creative material from a number of different sources. In any event, a file for clip art could save money for the church that does a good bit of direct mail.

A way to have an eye-catching advertising campaign at low cost was developed by a church in Texas. The Sunday School children were asked to put together sample ads they thought would interest people in coming to their church. They could use clip art, original drawings, or a combination of media. They had to work within the dimensions of a quarter page ad in a local weekly paper or in proportions enabling reduction to the mechanical requirements. From this program the church derived a series of clever, straightforward advertisements that attracted a good deal of attention in the community.

Some denominational communicators, also in Texas, developed a series of advertisements that proclaim in cartoon and attention-getting type the message of the church. The series can be ordered for a nominal fee and there is room within each ad for the church to insert its own name and address. (See Appendix.) The simple texts range from: "Heard a Whale of a Good Fish Story Lately? Ask Jonah." to "3 plus 2 equals 5: Not a Math Error But a Miracle" and "Each day we live is a miracle. Live it that way!" Other denominations offer their own series that can be utilized by local churches. The reproduction proofs of such ads are usually available, ready for printing at low cost. The newspaper can set the type for the church's name, address, and service times, or the communications chairperson can clip this information from some of its printed material, paste it carefully on the proof, and send it to the newspaper. It is necessary to ascertain, however, that the size of the ad conforms to the size of the space contracted for in the newspaper. If the ad is a bit smaller, a border can be drawn around it and it can be floated in the white space. If it is larger and is of approximately the right proportion, it can be reduced by the newspaper. The church will have to pay for the cost of reduction, but it will not amount to very much.

Many newspapers set aside space in their religious news sections for directories listing churches and services. Sometimes it is good to be listed in one of these, particularly if you are in a large city where you might be getting members from other parts of town. The cost would have to be weighed against the probable results. It might be well to query other churches currently advertising in this way. You might do it on a trial basis. One compelling reason to advertise in church directories or on church pages from time to time is that such revenue supports a church section in a newspaper, and without revenue the amount of space given to church news may shrink.

Other Print Communication: Brochures, Pamphlets, Direct Mail

When should a church undertake to produce a brochure? When should it go to professional printing services, forsaking its usual duplicating approach? What kind of response can be expected from direct mail?

When the budget committee begins to look at a request from the communications committee to do a brochure on some program of the church, they will probably demand the strongest possible argument for the request. Money is limited. New furniture is needed for the junior-high room. The lawnmower has broken down. Why do we need a brochure when we have all these other demands on our money?

A brochure may be justified:

1. When information on an upcoming event such as a seminar, retreat, or conference requires in-depth treatment.
2. When the viability of an event is dependent upon a certain attendance.
3. When an event is "brand new" in the life of the church and the community and is one which requires introductory information.
4. When the brochure could be used for other purposes as an informative piece on the church's educational programs to be included in an information kit for newcomers or when it could provide background to be used by participants in the event.
5. When the church has a program for which it hopes to acquire funding from a foundation or from a general fund-raising campaign.
6. As a commemorative project for a very special function—anniversary, milestone in the life of the church.

Brochures come in all kinds of forms, shapes, and sizes. Colors, die-cutting, color separations, special stock, special sizes and folds, can make even a small brochure costly. A brochure shaped like an airplane will cost a great deal more than a rectangular form with a picture of an airplane on it. Twenty-five brochures will cost you more per copy than 2500. There are many cost-cutting secrets that can help a church get the brochure it wants at minimum expense.

The most widely used and convenient form which costs the least money is the 5-½-by-8-½ single fold piece which can be stuck in a shirt pocket or mailed in a number ten envelope. It can be used as an insertion with a covering letter or even slipped into the church newsletter. Of course, the particular program or project to be communicated may demand a much larger pamphlet with illustrations and a heavy cover. For the present we will skip over these kinds of printed pieces in favor of the one of minimum cost.

Color
Your brochure need use only one color ink. If you want to achieve the effect of color, you can select a colored stock such as beige, grey, blue, green, or yellow. Stock should not be so dark as to make type unreadable. You may want to print your message in a colored ink which, so long as it is the only color used (including black), will still be classified as a single color and will not increase your price. More than one color means your mailer has to go back through the press a second time and therefore the price goes up.

Type
Type should be large—preferably black because that is the most readable—and well spaced so that it can be read quickly and easily. If you have a lot to say and can't sacrifice much space between lines, be sure to space out paragraphs. A page should not be so closed up that it looks gray to the casual eye. It may behoove you to cut the copy so that what you have to say makes more impact.

Art
Illustrations may be line drawings, which are cheapest because they can be pasted up on the flat along with the type and all shot at once by the printer. Halftones (photographs reproduced through a halftone screen for printing purposes) require another step. They have to be reduced or blown up (probably), made separately, and stripped onto the negative before the printing plate is made. If you have only a few halftones, they should not send the price up appreciably, but if you have many of varying sizes, be prepared to face considerable extra cost. Photos should be uncluttered, of simple background, clearly recognizable in small format. In our opinion, it is better to use a few photos and let them be large enough to be seen and appreciated. Many people want to cram in more photos than the format can hold with the result

that all have to be reduced drastically. No matter how much of a story you want to tell in this brochure, it is far better to tell it simply, to pick out highlights to write about and illustrate, than to throw everything into the pot at one time.

Variations

If you do not have access to drawings or photos, you can break up copy and impart interest and a pleasant feel through rules (use sparingly) and ornamental letters or by a variation in headline type. All-type brochures can be as interesting in their own way as those profusely illustrated. Here you have to make wise use of white space, keep the format clean and uncluttered, with just enough accent to make it look attractive. Generally, you should use no more than three type face variations in a small brochure and these variations should be within one type "family"—as Times Roman bold, italic, extra bold, medium. Too much variation tends to give what old-timers referred to as a "circusy" effect. If you don't know type, ask your printer. Look at examples of brochures he has done or show him an example of one you particularly like and ask him to follow that as much as possible with the material you plan to use. This is a good way to get a "ball park" price for a brochure before the work begins.

If you need to keep costs to a bare minimum, consider the one-page mailer. It can be set up like a newspaper article, with headlines and subheads. This format gives both urgency and authenticity to the material. It is recognizable; people have had experience with it. You can get a considerable amount of information into such a format. Don't print on both sides of the sheet unless the stock is quite heavy and opaque. Make a trial run by holding the paper in reading position. If the copy on the reverse side interferes at all with that on the front, forsake the idea of "two for the price of one."

If you are convinced that your project needs the services of a professional printer, be certain to get several bids on the job. This is time-consuming but well worth it. Be sure all the printers are bidding on exactly the same job—in terms of weight and type of paper stock, colors, amount of type set, number of copies run, folds, delivery. Two bids might show a wide disparity simply because one of them does not include folding, stapling and delivery, for example.

Do It Yourself

Investigate the possibility of saving some money by doing your own composition on an IBM typewriter. Typesetting is expensive, and even though you may

not have a machine which "justifies" (i.e., evens margins), a brochure may not demand such rigidity. You can line up the left-hand margin and let the right-hand margin come out however it will. If you have a great deal of copy to be "packed in" to the page, this would be very space consuming and would detract from the readability. In this case you have no choice but to have it set on a machine that justifies. IBM pica type may be reduced slightly to give a readable copy that is professional in appearance. Keep your copy "open" as much as possible by spacing between paragraphs or between subject blocks. Variations may be achieved by setting some copy narrower measure and letting it float or boxing it up to call particular attention to that part of the message. Such a segment could be done in italic or bold face (and with one of the newer ball-type typewriters you can make such a change without difficulty). For headlines, "set" your typewriter for All Caps or underline caps and lower case. Or you can buy transfer type in sheets at an art supply store, cut it out with an Exacto knife and transfer it to the page layout. Some fine blue lines on your sheet will give you a guide for lining it up and these will not be picked up in reproduction. A rounded wooden stick, such as a popsicle stick, is useful in getting the type to stick on your page.

Working with an Artist

For art work you can go several routes. The clip art from your file or from a clip-art service, as mentioned earlier, is a good source of illustration. Be sure not to use too many such illustrations. The mistake is often made of using a line illustration to introduce every new entry in the brochure in the belief that it calls attention to the copy. But there is a danger that if the page is too busy, nothing will be read and the eye will only be confused. There may be a talented person in the church who will do the pasteup. Or maybe someone who will draw some small cartoons or design some headlines freehand. If you feel the project requires the services of an artist, it might be well, as in the case of printers, to shop around. Some printers have a list of artists they will be glad to provide. Try a university, junior college, vocational-tech school. Ask the local weekly newspaper. Maybe their artist would like to do a bit of moonlighting. Go to whatever artist you select with a "rough"—that is, a sketched-out example of what you hope to produce, possibly an example of a printed piece you would like yours to resemble, and the amount of copy and illustrative material you plan on using. With these elements at hand, the artist can make suggestions and give you a price. Tell him or her frankly what your budget is. Maybe the artist will work with you.

To achieve the highest possible level of savings and still get a professional printing job, you would:

1. Write your own copy and take your own photos.
2. Set your own typewriter composition.
3. Do your own line illustrations.
4. Compose your own headlines using transfer type or typewriter.
5. Do your own camera-ready pasteup.

Pasteup

Phase 5 is where panic might well set in. What does this involve? Can anyone do it? If the piece is a simple four-page proposition with not too many fancy production ideas involved, the camera-ready pasteup can easily be accomplished by an amateur with only minimum equipment. A flat table. Tee square, triangle and rule. Dividers. Rubber cement. Eraser. Blue pencil. Scissors and Exacto knife. You save the cost of all the expensive interim steps by doing it yourself, reducing your final costs to those of making the negative, possibly some stripping (of halftones), plate for printing, paper stock, presstime (including folding). If the copy is to be shot the same size, space it out as it will be in the brochure with areas set aside for pasting down the line drawings, if any. Draw—with a steady hand—all rules and borders. For halftones, paste in "windows" the exact size as the picture in the finished brochure will be. The "window" can be a piece of dark red or black art paper. Be sure there is no "fuzz" on the edges. Art stores have special materials for making halftone windows. It's not expensive. You might inquire. Sizing a photo is not complicated, particularly if the printed photo is to be the same size as the original. If it is to be the same size as a cropped-out part of the original, simply mark your crop marks on the photo showing what is not to be used, measure it, and make the window the same size. Be sure to key photos to the windows, using letters or numbers, particularly if you are using several. If the photo is to be blown up or reduced, you will find it handy to use a proportioning scale that will show you what size the length and width of the photo must be in order to achieve the size requirements you need in the printed copy. For special effects such as screens, duotone, montages, surprinting, or whatever, ask your printer. If the job requires more expertise than he can give you over the counter, he will probably suggest the name of an artist.

As in the case of any task, the more you do camera-ready pasteup the easier it will become. There are a number of good books that are extremely helpful (see Appendix). The more that can be done within the church's communications structure, the more money can be saved on special printings. Whoever learns the techniques should also feel the responsibility for teaching someone else so that the church is never left without someone who can do the job. The main thing is to have the courage to try. It doesn't require that you be a professional as long as you stick with jobs that are relatively simple. Most church brochures and mailing pieces need not be slick or complicated. Fulfillment of purpose at the lowest possible cost is the usual criterion.

DIRECT MAIL

In this category we place letters, brochures, reprints, pamphlets, any printed or typed material to be mailed out by the church. "Please don't forget your pledge during the summer months. The church is never on vacation." As simple a postcard as that mailed to the congregation would be classified as a piece of direct mail. A letter from the bazaar committee asking for donations, outlining plans; a series of letters to newcomers and visitors; a quarterly report letter on the state of the church's health—all involve the church in this most important segment of the advertising field.

The three-piece mailing approach to back up the annual fund-raising effort of the church is a tried and true one. It involves three separate mailings by the chairperson of the campaign and/or the committee, spaced out so that there is at least a week in between and the last one is received no more than two days before the start of the personal visitation phase of the campaign. These mailings may be personal appeals in the form of direct letters from the drive's head. They may be combinations of a letter and an information brochure telling the recipient what the church hopes to do within the budget for which it asks support. A reprint of a supportive article may also be included—photo copying is cheap. Check possible copyright protection before you reprint even on a limited basis. It is not difficult to write a magazine or newspaper to get permission to reprint.

How do we get people to read letters? is a common question. It is true that most of us heave lap-loads of paper into the garbage every day. But if the church's direct mail piece is distinctive, i.e., has the church's logo on it for identification and some eye-catching introduction, the chances are it will be set aside with other mail for reading. Here remains the element of competition. The recipient may say, "Here's another letter from the church. I got one just like this last week," and throw it away. If the letter this week is on yellow stock (whereas last week's was on blue), it will immediately register as a new mailing. Sometimes a different way of folding, an envelope of a different color, some large, arresting headline on the outside will capture the reader's attention. One church, hoping to stimulate interest in its Vacation Church School, used bits and pieces of familiar images scattered about on the page. The caption was "We're going to put it all together." Noting the fish's head at the top of the page and the tail alongside paragraph four led the reader to to the conclusion that something different and intriguing was going on . . . well worth perusal!

Some rules of thumb for direct mail: Be short. Be neat. Make each piece, particularly in a series, as distinctive as possible. Don't be afraid of using original ideas, even if they're not professional.

If you are mailing a few pieces, use envelopes. Send first class. If the venture is vital to the life of the church and you are reaching beyond the church family, you might want to follow this same procedure. Always use the correct name and title of the person being addressed. A mailing for every member of the family or one per family? That depends. If you are going to use second-class mail under a permit, you might want to send one to everyone in the family. Should direct mail alone carry the weight of your campaign? Again, it depends on whom you are contacting. If the campaign is one in which others outside the church might participate, you may wish to use other media, including newspaper advertising and publicity.

The value of each of your mailings will double in proportion to the number of mailings you have. A major event should be preceded by at least two mailings—general information and a last-minute reminder. Mailings and phone calls in combination are most effective. It is easy to ignore a single mailing and it may not be worth its cost. Mailings should be part of other efforts even if they are in-church. Phone calls, bulletin notices, posters, and other types of communication may be used as well. Mailings are expensive and getting more so every year. Therefore, it is necessary to keep your mailing list up to date. Culling out those who are inactive or keeping several lists—one of "actives," one of both "actives" and "inactives," and still a third including visitors and prospects, is a good way of directing your mailing to where it will reach those from whom you wish a response. If you purchase a mailing list in order to get larger circulation for your message, be sure it is from a reliable source. If you have a large mailing to do, you might consider buying the list, having your envelopes stuffed and mailed for a turn-key price by a professional service. Small mailings may be done quite well at the church by volunteers.

Mailings with return forms are often effective. Requiring a response from the reader, one which will benefit him and the church, is a good way to increase the possibility that the material will be read. Giving the recipient a choice of options in returning the material is sometimes good. He can be told to mail the return coupon, bring it to church, give it to the committee chairman. Advertising professionals realistically do not expect more than a small return from any one mailing. But those who do return or respond to the effort will usually prove to be people you can count on for support of your project.

POSTERS/BULLETIN BOARDS

Posters draw attention far out of proportion to the investment required in producing them. Within the church are both the ability and the ingenuity to turn out attractive posters for use inside the church and even in the community. In this way, many churches advertise their bazaars, summer camping programs, vacation church school, special events. Often, making posters is the province of the younger grades of Sunday School. But that should not necessarily be the case all the time. Maybe the adults would like to make posters. Maybe several age groups would like to work together on one large poster. Posters give a church a festive air. Have you ever walked the hall of a high school prior to homecoming game? There is a definite air of excitement, much of it engendered by the large number of colorful posters hanging everywhere. Posters give the feel that something is going on. Posters, or banners strung overhead from stretched wire or cord, are certain of attracting attention.

Posters may be done on inexpensive lightweight board available at variety stores or supermarkets. They may be done using any medium and could involve several media—magazine cut-outs, fabric, water paints, photographs. To stimulate interest have a Best Poster Contest. For posters to be hung outdoors or in shopping centers you may wish to get heavier board from an art supply store. A poster should have a central theme. It should be able to be read and comprehended in a short space of time, have a strong element on which to focus and a minimum of copy. You may get an art teacher from your area school system to come one Sunday and talk to the church school on the basics of making posters.

The church bulletin board is a good place for communication. In order to be of interest it must be changed frequently, look neat, be organized. The bulletin board that still has yellowed clippings about last year's events won't be looked at very often or very seriously. Hang on your board letters of thanks and notes from traveling members, notices of meetings coming up, notices of events going on in other area churches, calls for assistance on projects, prayer lists, flower lists, a chart of the progress in a fund drive, a drawing of a proposed new building. It should be a veritable newspaper of the church, reflecting its active life. Visitors often judge churches by what they see on bulletin boards. From a quick glance they can decide whether the life of this church is stimulating and interesting.

The decision on how much communication to do, when and through what media to do it, depends largely on the audience you are trying to reach (as well as on the money you have to spend).

The following is a checklist which may help in making that kind of decision:

Other considerations:
- Is this a series of events?
- An information campaign?
- An action campaign (to get people to do something)?

If the latter, you may want to mix media, using telephone, direct mail, newspaper publicity, as well as congregational promotional facilities. Will the return be sufficient to absorb the cost of the promotion? Does your budget include an honorarium for the speaker, speaker's expenses, renting of special equipment, advertising and printing? When money is being spent off the top, there will be a definite need to include an advertising and publicity budget to insure enough attendance to satisfy these expenses.

Audience to be reached	Church bulletin	Posters/ Bulletin board	Direct mail	Bulletin stuffers	Phone	Weeklies	Dailies	Radio	TV
Active Congregation	X	X		X	X				
Active/Inactive	X		X	X	X				
Immediate Community		X				X		X	
Small town/towns						X		X	
Metropolitan area						X	X	X	X
Special audience			X						

CHAPTER TWELVE

Radio: Air Waves to Another Congregation

- Has your church ever used radio? Why not?
- Do you know what a radio spot is? How to write one?
- Have you ever visited any radio station?
- Do you know who is responsible for news on radio?
- Have you ever given any thought to the audience you might be able to deliver and how you could deliver it?
- Do you ever talk about radio programming in your church, including the possibilities of being actively involved in radio?
- Do you consider radio an opportunity to promulgate concerns and viewpoints of the church or merely as a means of publicizing a specific event?

It would be surprising to have a head count of the number of churches that would answer negatively to all of these questions. Radio is for someone else, not for a local church. It's for the churches in the big cities, the churches who have big budgets, the ecumenical groups, the adjudicatories. Not for the small or medium sized church in the suburbs, in the small town, or on the fringes of downtown, or in the middle of downtown.

USING RADIO

It is also surprising to find out how many church people don't think radio is worth the effort. Who listens? Radio is a has-been. But actually, more Americans than ever before are listening to radio. More than 150 million sets are in use and a high percentage of these are in use during that important period known as "drive time" when Americans are plowing back and forth to home and work via some freeway or other. Here is the ultimate in captive audiences, as you know if you've ever been stuck in an hour or more long traffic jam. The portability of radio has also boosted its popularity as the leisure time companion of millions—it fits into such popular pursuits as fishing and hunting, camping and hiking, even biking. Any public medium so continuously listened to inevitably becomes the concern of the church whose business is to reach out to people wherever they may be.

We heard recently of a medium-sized (800 members) church in Arkansas whose experience in radio provides a good example of what can be done without professional resources but with creativity and enthusiasm.

This church sponsored a 13-week experimental radio ministry with a weekly half-hour show aired at 6:15 P.M. every Monday. It was a kind of religious magazine of the air, hosted by the minister of the originating church and later joined by individuals and groups from other churches. A typical broadcast called for opening and closing religious music of various types, a review of the church's weekly calendar of services and activities, a prayer for our nation, a short-course lesson: How the Bible was first translated into English. Who was St. Francis of Assisi? A Bible feature or reading. A feature on the history or organization or belief of the denomination represented by the sponsoring church. Special announcements, such as the securing of a new minister or a taped conversation with first-graders talking about what they think evangelism is. Also, there were taped interviews with church and community leaders on current topics, a replay of portions of the worship service, and the broadcasting in headline fashion of worldwide religious news.

The broadcasts concentrated on content. Those committed to the process became enthusiastic about learning production needs and techniques. The hardest task turned out to be getting members of the congregation into the habit of tuning in each Monday evening.

The church had three goals for the project:

1. To broaden communication with the church family.
2. To reach the outside world with news of the denomination and the church.
3. To present to the community interesting and worthwhile religious programming.

The sponsors expressed satisfaction that the ministry fulfilled all three objectives.

As a model that seems to prove the point: religious programming on radio is possible for average churches. Religious programming need not be dull. Religious programming can fit very well into the objectives of the church whether it be under the heading of evangelism, Christian Education, stewardship, or all three.

The church is into every aspect of life. The church is God's people wherever they are, standing in the midst, and it is not inappropriate or factitious for the church to speak on anything that touches the lives of its people.

That is the broad picture. Where does your church or my church fit in? The steps are simple but may not lead you to the desired objective overnight since much spade work must be done before it's time to appear at the radio station with a solid proposal.

Radio and TV stations are required by the FCC (Federal Communications Commission) to give a certain percentage of their time to voluntary civic and charitable groups. Most stations exceed the required time. Regardless, they are under regular scrutiny by the FCC, are subject to complaint by individuals through the FCC, and must comply if they are to have their licenses renewed. So, as a nonprofit voluntary group, the church is not asking for anything that is not available to it or to which it is not entitled.

How to Begin

The first task is to develop interest in a radio ministry within your congregation. This can be done in a number of ways. Listening to the fare that is currently being aired on one or two local stations may stimulate your people to want to do better or equally well, just as the budding novelist is inspired by reading a book he feels he can easily surpass. The purpose of being in radio may be another aspect of a group communications study. The broadcast media are monopolized by a great lot of manipulators—but manipulators for what? For gain, for self-aggrandizement, for power, for promulgation of various secular activities that are not in the least lofty and may often, from a moral standpoint, be barely acceptable. Doesn't the church also have its duty in that world? The church is called in faith to stride forth from its historic shell trusting in the power of the Holy Spirit to lead it into new ways of communicating the truth. The more the whole church can be brought to an understanding of this obligation the easier the task of getting into the broadcast media will be.

The second step is to bring as much of the church as possible into the decision making: What kind of offering will we make, who will do it, what will be involved? Who will give time and who will give money? The communications organization of the church can serve as the nucleus for refining the information, collecting ideas, setting up the human resources that will be needed, formulating the step-by-step process for bringing the project to fruition.

With urban centers having upwards of 50 radio stations in operation at various times of the day and night, it's important to consult the telephone directory or Chamber of Commerce listing in your area to get a description of the stations in your broadcast range. A "hard rock" station may not be closed to religious programming but it would certainly require material with a different approach than a station with "country" and "classical" fare. Stations aimed at particular racial and ethnic groups also abound. Some stations broadcast only news and weather; some only music. The radio "marketplace" is clearly defined, and part of the homework of any church group entering here is to determine what audience they hope to reach and which station directs itself to that audience. And even given these distinctions, there are other factors radio surveys have uncovered about the listening audience: it changes every 15 minutes; from 5 to 10 A.M. and from 3 to 7 P.M. is radio's "prime time"; talk shows are heavily scheduled midday because this is "at-home" audience time.

An early call on a radio station or two will facilitate planning. Make this an informal visit to discover how the station operates, what the opportunities for churches might be, who the station personnel are. It should be a goodwill visit with some positive things flowing from the visiting team, who we hope are well steeped in the techniques of active listening. You will probably meet the program director, the station manager, the news director, the public service director. In some stations these may be combined duties. The theme of the first visit should be: becoming acquainted, and how can we help. It should be made known from the outset that you have people to reach, perhaps an impressive number, and you would like to help radio to reach them. The idea of a ready-built block audience is always of interest to a commercial station even though they may give you free time. They sell their commercial time to advertisers on the basis of number of listeners (and this may be at a rate of up to $100 a minute).

The station may outline a number of possibilities for you to consider. These may include:

1. Spot announcements (public service) telling of specific events.

2. Community calendar news (many stations have a designated block of time for these tidbits).

3. News on regular news broadcasts.

4. Providing a resource person for a call-in show, "Ask the Expert," or some other kind of specialty feature.

5. Participating in an interview or conversation show.

6. Filling a block of time on Sunday morning with a broadcast of part or all of a service (this time is generally purchased time and will cost you anywhere from $150 to $300 or more a month).

7. Filling a block of time with a sermon or church music. This also, depending on the format offered, may be considered commercial time which must be paid for.

8. An original show which may assume the format of the "Magazine of the Air," as described earlier, may involve teens, music, interviews, or any one of a number of elements. This should be planned and ready to go, with guests all lined up for a 13-week segment before it is seriously offered to the station as a sustaining program. Another possibility is the packaging of the church's own commercial program by buying up a block of time and either getting people within the church to sponsor it or selling spots to businesses outside the church. Open conversation with station personnel will pinpoint possibilities of this type and will probably provide good guidelines in developing whatever project you decide upon.

Radio Spots

We have previously covered the writing of radio spots in connection with a single church event. If nobody in the church knows how to write spots and there is little interest in learning, you can begin to develop both interest and capability by giving one of the Church School classes the problem of reading news stories (probably in a church paper) and getting them to boil these down in spots of 50–75 words (30 seconds), 150–175 words (one minute). This is good training and can be fascinating to a group that's never tried it before. Be prepared for such comments as "Hey, this is easy!" "I didn't even know I could write!" "Let's get into radio!"

Spots can also cover other aspects of churchgoing or church understanding. You might feature different religious seasons, what they mean, how to observe them. A broader series featuring various denominations in your town and something not well known about each one, "Did you know this about this church?" This could be done with one voice (you select and tape), a professional voice (taped or live), or a series of taped voices representing the churches involved. If you spearhead, remember your responsibility is auditioning, selecting voices, and getting everybody to the taping session on time. Recently, a great series of spots was made on different age and interest levels in one large church, each person introducing himself or herself and telling why he or she felt it important to "be" in church on Sunday. The youngest was a child of five who, with his tremendous innocence and charm, was an immediate hit throughout the listening area. This range of individuals could be used to address attention to a variety of topics: What the church means to me. Why I am a Baptist, Methodist, Episcopalian, etc. If you have in a series a small child, a teen-ager who uses "today's" language, a successful lawyer, a housewife, a business woman, a school teacher, a retiree, a grandmother—the list is endless—you get a broad range of viewpoint which can be healthy for one church or all churches.

News

Some stations have special religious news sections in which you are welcome to participate. Many of these are aired on Saturday morning. Some are daily airings. They may be 15 to 30 minutes. They may wrap around an interview or an in-depth news feature. The most obvious answer to the question, "Why wasn't our church's program on the news?" is that nobody ever thought to send it in. Send in announcements (brief) of these kinds of news: new minister or staff person coming, important speaker, new group organized, new church building or expansion, participation in community project, unusual missionary work, largest-in-history (this could be Easter service, revival service, confirmation class, etc.), young people's activity, senior's activity, church revival, bazaar, fair. There is today much interest in:

1. *Youth:* Drugs, alcoholism, education, sports, culture, social behavior.
2. *Seniors:* Social activities, loneliness, financial support, contributions.
3. *Singles:* Loneliness, raising children, finding new identity.
4. *Women:* Liberation, employment, politics.
5. *Young married:* Economic struggles, family problems.

What the church is doing in all of these areas is news of importance to the community and therefore to local radio. Follow the station's guidelines. Broad-spectrum news can go out as a routine to all radio stations in your area. If you are working with one station on a news story more in depth, or on one that involves a viewpoint, give that station an exclusive.

Resource for Call-in or Ask the Expert

The church has expertise in many areas in which the station is already deeply involved: Family counseling, stewardship, community betterment, youth problems. The church is actively involved in many areas in which the community is also participant. This will be quite appealing to the station—the offer of an expert, either on the church's staff or from the congregation, who can bring the Christian viewpoint to bear on a significant problem. You might have a lawyer who would talk on common-law marriages, a doctor on abortion, a psychologist on child abuse.

In this instance you must think beyond congregation or denomination, beyond the churches to those others out there. It's not the same as preaching a sermon or directing a class where all who are listening already believe. You must have some idea of how you would like people outside the church to see the church, through its works, its areas of social and human concern, to see it within its pure sense as offering accessibility to God, within its working sense as laborer in the human vineyard.

There are many ways in which people "see" the church. Through its congregation and its leaders, its history and tradition, its active internal programs, its missionary work and social programs "outside," its acceptance of responsibility in every aspect of life—

schools, community safety, politics, community development, recreation, culture, employment, etc. Through radio you have a rare opportunity to bring people to a new vision of the church by expressing as much of the church's life as possible whenever there is an opportunity. This doesn't mean preaching a sermon. It means responding in a thoughtful manner with information that reflects the church truly and deeply.

Original Show

If it's good enough, the station may take it on as a sustaining program. Or a way may have to be found by the church to buy the time, and perhaps recoup by selling spots within it.

The program itself might follow any number of formats. It could be a "think" time, using bits from cassettes from various sources (national denominational headquarters, publishing firms, the communications or Christian Education offices of denominations which generally offer a variety of cassettes). You could use the tape or tapes as the central point of the show, followed by a panel or conversational follow-up dissecting or amplifying the contents of the tape. It is important to remember that the follow-up must add to the taped material rather than being a repetition of it. If your panel members look at the subject from opposing viewpoints, so much the better. Too many panel members or conversationalists may spoil the show, add confusion. Too many voice sounds are babel. Radio is very much a one-to-one medium in which the listener wants to be able both to identify, and identify with, the people he is hearing. Let's say you have three—yourself and two others—for the discussion. Dissect the tape. Call each other by name. Build on the tape to send the discussion even further. Then you might open the lines for call-in material. Or you might have a resource person to comment on the tape. You might end with a bibliography of meetings and readings where people could get further information on the same subject.

Things to Remember:

Though you don't need a "name brand" personality as a show headliner, you should have people with credentials. If you don't want to use a professional tape, use your professional resource person as the center around which the program functions. Set up everything in time blocks. Get time commitments for rehearsal and taping. Appoint a coordinator to see that it all happens. Bring an audience (if you can) for the taping or live sessions if the show is to be done that way.

The Dichotomy:

A hard controversial subject directly, but not necessarily, concerning the church: a matter of justice, politics, women's rights. Two people on each side to discuss some aspect of the subject from opposing views. Or the opposition might evolve from the kinds of people you use: Kids and parents—very candid; senior citizens seeking work, and employers; alcoholics and nonalcoholic members of their families; teens questioning alcoholics or drug users. You could get a 13-week series going without difficulty. One show a week, fifteen minutes or maybe thirty. You can use this format to uncover myths, debunk popular theories, show the church's strength and concern. Another route is to have politicians, doctors, women's advocates, all representatives of recognized social strata to be questioned on some aspect of their lives. High-school students questioning politicians about ethics; women asking questions of doctors on abortion or the high cost of medical services; wage earners asking bankers about interest rates and money lending practices. The main thing here is that the line of questioning represent those questions that the audience might be asking were it given a similar opportunity.

The Mechanics:

You need relaxed people. Good voices. Enthusiasm. A variety of phrases and pauses. Paced delivery. Emphasizing of key words and phrases. Change of pitch and pace occasionally. Friendly informality. Avoid people who repeat common word crutches such as "you know" or "what I mean is" or even "uh."

Practice your group. Have home recording sessions in one of your church's classrooms. This may tell you in short order whether you have something that's ready for professional presentation. Then you can audition for the station. Remember they can still turn you down on the grounds that you're not good enough. So it will take some preparation, some homework.

In interviewing avoid yes or no questions. Head nodding is just another form of silence. Be sure your guests understand the time limit, hand signals (slow down, speed up, one minute left, break, etc.). Be sure they know the need to be clear, the need to be specific. Give your guests a route but not a script. Don't let them wander too far from the main topic. Use questions that can be answered in terms of how or what or why. Break big overhead questions into more specific ones. If the interview time is nearing an end give clues: "We have time for just one more quick question." Reserve the last ten or fifteen seconds for a closing remark and a thank you.

Religious News Roundup:

You are the producer. What's going on around the churches? This must not be just a list of bazaars and seminars. You can get into depth on two or three things using a guest. An approach we have heard used on some stations calls for the guest's voice on tape addressing himself to three or four specific aspects of the subject. The host's voice, live, leads into the response which then comes on taped. It is very much like a live interview but much more compact. Alternatively you might want to feature one interview (live or taped) and some music followed by quick appearances of guests telling what specifics they are into—teens, seniors, etc. You might get 10 or 15 minutes weekly for this.

Panel:

You can use the same panel members each week with an additional new one or a special guest. As host, you introduce the panel and the subject, open with a lead question, and make sure all members participate. It is also the host's job to take the show off the air. To get maximum mileage out of a panel situation, get a true back-and-forth discussion going within the panel, avoiding a "you throw, panel bats, you throw again" box. Interaction is the key to a successful panel. So is spontaneity.

You could use a panel-plus-authority. The authority speaks briefly. The panel questions, not to tear down but to amplify and expand what has been said. It's a little like "Meet the Press." This could be done with church figures and local news people. The host or moderator keeps the discussion moving, providing an ambience for open expression of views. The authority should be presented in the context of some current question or situation.

Friendly Debates:

Firing Line has been on television for some years. It is an example of a successful format. The host is acerbic and shrewd, the guests are generally people who are themselves interesting or who are conversant with interesting subject matter. The host gives a platform, not to stir up controversy but to examine it. A little heat is good but you don't want a raging personality conflagration. In the last few moments the host sums up and thanks people. In this format, guests are told ahead of time what the show's rules are. Each guest (if there is more than one) has an opening block of time to present his case. The discussion continues in the form of probing questions and requests for clarification. This can be varied by having studio audience questions or call-ins. In the case of the latter, the station should have facilities for recording and delaying playback in order to screen out material which would be inappropriate. Or the call can be received by the host and presented by him to the audience and the guest. "A listener from Hartford wants to know. . . ." This takes some of the live edge off the calling process but it provides better control. The host and the guest can open the show, bat the controversy about for a bit, then invite comment.

Variety Show:

This would involve several people in a deep commitment which would demand large amounts of time and activity. A good deal of planning, scheduling of guests, and rehearsing would be called for. A flexible format for such a show could go like this:

1. Host opens with greetings and comments. Possibly introductory music.
2. Presentation of highlights of the week around the churches.
3. National news headlines on religion—The Religion Front.
4. Historic background on the season of the year or some big event in the church's history (something like the Bicentennial Minute).
5. A guest of interest. Someone who sings or plays an instrument. Or someone who has an interesting story to tell; a personal experience, perhaps.
6. Closing announcements—upcoming events.

Music could flow through this format. Segments of drama could be used. Variety is the strong point. Repetitive introductory ID's would give the program a block feeling: "And Now . . . This Week in Religion . . ." with a music tag.

Drama:

A big order. Probably expensive since you would need to go into intensive rehearsal, probably buy scripts, perhaps pay actors. Working with the drama department of a university or high school could be one way of cutting through some of the expense, but the church would probably lose control of the material. A large church has some possibility of doing this kind of thing successfully. When drama is an ongoing part of church life and a group is at home in the medium, radio drama becomes a short and very appropriate step. A drama that has been produced successfully in the church may be appropriate almost "as is" for radio. Other churches may have similar groups so it may be possible to work up a series of church dramas for Saturday afternoon presentation, for example. Scripts suitable for radio presentation may be obtained from national workshops, so it is a matter of casting and producing it within the church. There is a dearth of good children's drama on radio and the church has an opportunity to step into this gap with some good offerings.

Disk Jockey:

An all-religious disk jockey program may be a possibility, though the demand by stations for such a presentation may be limited. If you have a talented person who can do this kind of thing effortlessly, there is certainly no end to good religious music, much of which has strong popular appeal. Church music today runs the gamut from rock-beat "message" music to Handel's *Messiah* and the Mormon Tabernacle Choir. Gospel rock, Gospel country, and progressive Gospel are all authentic types of music on today's scene and there is plenty of audience out there for them. If you don't have a DJ to offer, you might approach one of your local stations about doing an all-church-music DJ program using one of their people. Promise support. If the station decides to go along with the idea, go out and dig up response. Fifty to a hundred people a week calling in and saying "That's great," "We like the show," "Keep it up" will assure the program a long and happy life. An important part of the church's job of communication is responding to the media in a positive way when that kind of response is merited.

CHAPTER THIRTEEN

Television: Is It a Medium for the Church?

Some of the largest TV viewing audiences ever polled have been those watching live appearances of Evangelist Billy Graham or in earlier days of television, Msgr. Fulton J. Sheen. In both of these cases the church was indeed communicating and to the widest possible audiences.

How can the small church hope to get into such a heady arena, to use a medium so sophisticated and powerful that it pervades every aspect of American life and occupies most of us during large portions of our daily lives? Is television after all so expensive and necessitating of such expertise that church communicators should not even regard using it as a possibility?

The question of whether or not churches should concern themselves with the use of television is much more complex than similar questions about other media. There is little difficulty getting into print or radio. Slides and audio tape can be made handily. But getting into television—even though there may be a variety of entrance doors—often poses problems.

FORMS AND APPROACHES

TV is available in a number of forms and offers a variety of approaches, some of which are within reach of smaller congregations, and some of which are, because of the expense required in using them or preparing for them, available only to well-funded churches, large denominational bodies, ecumenical or co-op groups. But there are ways in which even small churches can enter into television without heavy expenditure or involvement of large numbers of personnel.

In one sense all churches, large or small, urban or rural, can use television as a medium of communicating with today's world. They do this by studying television programming—from soap operas and movies to commercials and news—and drawing from it whatever applications of the Christian Gospel it may present. Much material lacks any such application, a condition which of itself suggests critical studies and responsible communication with networks and/or local producers or sponsors. The church has tremendous power to make television "clean up its act," and much that has already been done has come about because of responsible prodding of the networks to produce better programs and by creative responses in opposition to inferior or unsuitable material. One of the major results has been the protection of children from unsuitable material during times when they constitute a major part of the audience. Other less spectacular results have come about because Christians, either individually or collectively, have expressed concern.

We will be dealing in this chapter first of all with how the church can become an active participant in television generally, including local programming, public broadcasting, network, and cable.

Briefly we would mention an obvious route: the outright purchase of local broadcast time either for weekly church services, a series of special programs, or a one-time-only program featuring a live event of major significance such as a revival. You will find, glancing at the Sunday listings, that most church-sponsored time is aired between the hours of 7 A.M. and 3 P.M. A large percentage of this is local and involves direct presentation of the Gospel message through music and preaching or live services from major churches. Religious air time is devoted almost exclusively to these kinds of presentations, a situation which precludes using much of the tremendous creative potential that lies within congregations all over America. Since this is paid television, available locally at costs ranging upwards from $250 for 30 minutes, it is obviously only feasible for churches enjoying substantial financial support. Though this may be viewed as outreach or evangelism by the sponsoring body, it is a fact that much of this kind of programming reaches mainly shut-ins or immobile people, including the elderly, and thus can be regarded as an extended service of a very specialized nature rather than an offering which will further the work of the church or give an expanded image of who worshipping Christians are. Since church dollars in most cases must be unreasonably stretched to cover all demands, there is little opportunity along the route of paid religion for the vast majority of American congregations. They are therefore obliged to substitute creativity and ingenuity for money. We hasten to add that there are numbers of churches in the land that are fortunate to have both.

Broadcast TV

Let us look for a moment at the possibilities for churches in local programming over broadcast TV. To figure at all in the local television scene it is essential that the Christian body be aware of what is being offered in the way of programming and how the church might work within that situation or add to and enhance it. How do you go about getting the facts about how much time is allotted to religion in a local situation? You, as a member of the public and coowner of the public airways, are entitled to ask a TV station to show you programming statements and their license renewal application status. Under Federal Communications Commission regulations, the license of every station must be renewed annually and is subject to being challenged by any member of the public. Though most of us are dimly aware of the public nature of the airways, the value of this situation to ourselves may escape us; few of us seem to realize that if a station is not doing a good job in our area, we have powerful and effective recourse. Usually, however, it doesn't get to that point. You will find that most TV stations are open and willing to show you their records and discuss programming with you. If you wish to take copies of the public record with you for further study, you have but to ask. The station is obligated to provide, for a reasonable fee, copies of the pages you need.

Here is something the communications committee can get its teeth into. How many hours on Sunday are devoted to religion? How much of that is local? How much is paid? How many hours on other days are given to religion? How does this compare with the total hours of programming? With public service programming? How much network religion is being aired? How much of this is paid and how much is public service or a sponsored special event? Where are local public service spots shown? A six months' study with emphasis on local programming would be a project of sufficient duration to involve listening to and critiquing some of the offerings and sharing responses. Determination to get into the picture and to offer something unique and valuable to a public medium could be one result of such a study. Certainly the committee will come away with a better understanding of how religious programming is accomplished in their community. Relationships between church and TV station can be constructed as the result of the study. The committee may even, as a part of its work, invite a representative of the station to appear before them to speak and to answer questions. Most stations are happy to send someone in response to such requests. There should be adequate lead time so that the appearance can be scheduled. A follow-up thank you letter to the station's management will cement good relations and provide a useful basis for future contacts.

The study may reveal that there is a certain amount of programming in which the church does or can play a role. This may include locally produced interviews, issues, or magazine format shows. Also news analysis programs. Anything that fits into one of these or similar categories can be expected to be a possibility for church participation. Are issues being aired in which churches have a stake? Is the Christian viewpoint being expressed? Is the church, as the church, being given an opportunity to present itself in any way? The church most certainly should be represented in public affairs programs, or wherever problems of people are under discussion. The work of the church is an ingredient in the community mix and is entitled to be shown as such.

If the church is being represented by a spokesperson, do those views responsibly represent the Christian community? If not, it may be time to speak out.

Steps Toward Incentive

Often in a local situation—because it is easier, thought to carry more weight, and even in some cases is safer—the TV station will continually tap persons from a select handful of clergy or laity. Other churches, watching from the sidelines, have no incentive to develop potential from within their own ranks.

How can such a situation be changed? Step One is knowing what is going on, who is being used, what kinds of views are expressed. Do you have people in your church whose knowledge and ability equals those of the "public figures" who appear day after day, week after week, representing the Christian viewpoint in your community? Are your people speaking out on issues? Are they deeply involved in the local scene? A small church can flex power far beyond budget or numbers because of talented, interested, community-minded people. Today's concerned Christians serve in a variety of community positions, ranging from school board to city government. Step Two is seeking these people out so that they can be brought to the attention of the media in your community in effecting TV programming changes.

Step Three is the bringing-together process: people and station. You may have the issue, something that has not yet been aired, and the "pro" to speak to it. By now you know the station personnel and the opportunities. You will feel free, as a member of the communications committee, to call and suggest an issue or a speaker.

Should your study of local programming indicate there is a genuine need for more light on public issues or perhaps a new approach, you might want to reach into your church's own supply of talent and come up with people to provide the ongoing anchorage or focal point for a new series. This will require time and dedication. If people willing to give these are available, the next task is to get them together and develop a format using their unique gifts to the best advantage.

Questions and Concerns

There are certain questions you must first ask yourself and your communications group so that you will be prepared to deal with the questions and concerns of the TV station. Addressing yourselves to these early on will minimize those remaining when you finally get to the point of negotiating with the TV people. This kind of preparation will require meeting and paperwork. It can be a natural outgrowth of the study you have previously made of existent programming in your community. Consider these questions in the early stage of deliberation:

1. Can the idea be translated into (a) a single show, (b) several shows, (c) a segment of an ongoing show?
2. If it is to be a new and independent offering, do you have a short memorable name in mind for it, one that will attract attention in newspaper listings that will lend itself to publicity?
3. Whom do you see as your audience? Families? Children? Women?
4. What would be your suggested day and time for airing? This, of course, would have to fit with local programming requirements.
5. Why do you think people will watch?
6. Is the program of a type that will readily build a loyal following? Are there possibilities for feedback?

The "selling" part of your work will be convincing the TV station of the reliability and professionalism of your people, of the depth of your commitment to the task no matter how long it may be. You will have to give assurances of commitment to rehearsal schedules as well. You will have to be convincing in your enthusiasm for the expertise and authority of the people who will be the backbone of your program. If you foresee special appearances during the series by guests, statements of interest and assurance of availability from them would be most desirable. You will want to have your ideas on paper with a sample program worked out in some detail. What will you need in the way of studio space, props, visual aids, film? Will you need to do any part of the program on location?

The second round of questions—or it could be the first, depending on how audience-hungry the TV station is at the time you appear—concerns the viewers. How many do you feel you can deliver? A denominational block in your community could be considerable. Find out just how big it is and have that figure handy. How much promotion are you prepared to do? An outline of promotion plans, professionally prepared, could not help but be a major asset in selling your idea. Will your church work with local newspapers, put out posters, request all area churches to use promotional material in their newsletters? Will the church place advertising in the local papers? Will there be a person specifically in charge of all promotion? The more thoroughly you appear to have studied all these concerns the easier it will be to catch the genuine interest of the station. How about evaluation? Any plans for making a survey of audience response once the program is launched? There should be an overall strategy of which marketing (promotion) and evaluation should be part.

The initial presentation requires considerable courage because of the size of the investment in time and work. It is nothing to be entered into lightly because what had begun as a new and joyful experience could easily turn out to be a heavy personal burden for somebody. Over against the commitment should be placed the value. The work must be considered as a

A church can have its own TV-type panel discussions.

community ministry from which many people benefit. As a work of evangelism it will reach many of the unchurched as well as some who are prospects for the particular sponsoring church. The church will be seen by the public not as a persuader or as assault troops in a head-on evangelistic confrontation but as a participant in the daily life of human beings, speaking to and working through the problems of today's world. Granted, this requires skillful people bringing the church's message to the world, not only as biblical Christians and believers but as knowledgeable human beings involved in the process of living confidently and radiantly. In this sense the church may come across more authentically than it does within its traditional form. Those people directly involved in the effort are doing Christian work in a powerful and vital way.

Many churches simply do not have creative people willing to commit themselves to a 13- or 26-week TV schedule. However, there may be one-timers who will speak on specific subjects, and these should be sought out, their credentials made known to the communications committee, and their experience and knowledge made use of whenever possible. A list of such people and their expertise and availability could be sent to the local TV stations for their files. From time to time there should be personal follow-up. "Do you need a particular authority? Do you think you will need such an

expert in the future? In a current series on child abuse, would you consider the testimony and expertise of Dr. Smith? She would be willing to appear, and she probably knows more about the subject than anybody in the city. I would be glad to get her together with you so that you could work something out." Be helpful, be friendly, let the station take the lead in telling you what it would like to do on the matter. After that your job is to make it possible.

Beyond this there are other ways in which local churches can enter television. There are the daily news shows which, from time to time, feature events in the church such as well-known visitors and speakers making appearances there. "How about an interview? Would you be interested in covering this event?" Don't hit them with every usual or purely in-church activity you have going. The communications committee should study their year calendar and earmark certain activities as possible for TV coverage.

If it is known three weeks in advance that Robert X, a missionary who has served in Africa and has recently been in one of the independent nations where the church is or has been threatened, is coming to speak at one of your Sunday services, a number of questions must be answered as quickly as possible. How long will he be in town? Will he be available to speak on local radio or TV and, if so, when? What are his other commitments? Early contact of a guest's office will get you this type of information as well as an up-to-date biography and a photo, including recent data about his African experiences. As soon as you have his schedule, you will want to call one or more local TV stations. If they have a panel or a new interview show in their lineup and it fits in with his schedule, you might offer your guest for that spot. Or you could have him at the station for interview at a certain time. Perhaps the station would want to cover his talk at the church or interview him there. You may want a press conference (see chapter five, "The Press Conference"). The main thing is that a responsible communications person from the church calls with background on the speaker and offers to set up something. One or more stations will quite likely be interested. If you do succeed in setting up an interview, you might want to ask the station about acquiring a copy of the video tape. This could be played back for your church or as a community event involving other churches and the general public. It could provide the focal point for an adult study program. Such requests can usually be worked out rather easily.

What are some other news possibilities? How about an anniversary homecoming? Two visitors from Bangkok and a 97-year-old woman who still does needlepoint. Dedication of a new building. Is there a "space capsule" cornerstone with memorabilia? What is interesting about the building? The architect? the fund-raising effort? Unusual event. Blessing of the pets. Planting of a memorial tree. Settting off helium-filled balloons with tickets to publicize a bazaar-barbecue. A traditional festival involving an authentic activity of the area. A youth film workshop. A parade. Bikeathon. All of these have to be examined in relation to other church events, including those covered recently. How unusual or outstanding is this specific event? How much coverage has your church received recently on local news programs? But if in doubt, ask. Offer to do all the leg work necessary in procuring background information, setting up dates and times, getting commitments. A person who is both willing and professional is usually such a refreshing experience that a TV station will bend over backwards to work out something for the church he or she represents.

When a TV crew is sent out to take a few segments at an event, the church as a whole must be prepared and cooperative. This may involve reserved parking for equipment trucks, help with cable placement, rearranging furniture, distribution of lighting, handling traffic—both human and automotive. There is a certain amount of inconvenience involved in such coverage but the results are almost always well worth it.

If you genuinely feel that a forthcoming event is TV material, it would be well to contact the station reasonably well in advance, giving background and offering cooperation. Three weeks prior to the event, if possible, is a good time to begin inquiry. "We are planning. . ." and give a brief description. "We would like to have coverage on the evening news if possible or. . . . (leave it open)." The station might offer to interview one of the principals in advance of the event on a local news-interview show. This would give ample time.for such arrangements to be made.

Planning is the key to all good TV relationships. Willingness to follow through is a must. Beyond that, an aptitude for what is newsworthy and of genuine interest to the larger community is an asset of inestimable value, one which can be developed through study and concern.

If an event requires the services of a commentator, you might be fortunate enough to have assigned to it someone employed by the station who is also a member of your denomination. If you know of such a person, you should feel perfectly free to suggest him or her. Or there may be someone in your congregation who has TV or radio background—either currently or from the past—and who is also knowledgeable about the event. Such a person's services might be most acceptable to the station.

During the event, mini interviews with people who are involved in it, might be arranged. This will require the services of the communications committee whose job it will be to help brief the interviewee and solidify arrangements for place and time of interview. One great result of TV coverage: the whole church will be excited by its media experience. The effect of it will reach the whole community and its benefits will undoubtedly be felt by the congregation for some time to come.

An average 30-minute, twice-a-day TV news show devotes anywhere from 7 to 12 minutes to sports and weather news. Your news segment may be compressed into one minute. You have to pick somebody (if you have that choice) to get the message over clearly and succinctly. Some things are not strictly news but are nevertheless timely and of news interest. These may include the commemoration of a religious holiday or celebration of a season. You might research out some local observance that is of particular interest, if not from your church or denomination, from a Christian neighbor whose enactment of the event will tell the Christian story for all the community's churches.

If you have spot news—and it's not of an emergency nature, such as the church catching on fire or being robbed—call the facts in to the TV station as soon as possible after it has taken place. Most stations have roving units with mini cameras that can give on-the-spot coverage.

The more you talk to station people without being demanding or verbose, the more you reveal to them how much audience your church and religion in general in your community can reach, the more you will tend to figure in their programming plans and the more they will call on you when they think of religious news and features.

Public service opportunities are plentiful but there is also a big demand on them, particularly in the larger cities. If your own city has one TV station and only one church of your denomination, you might expect to be able to get public service representation occasionally. In a large city there are countless calls on the amount of time the station devotes to religious matters as part of its overall public service. Here again, your relations with the station will stand you in good stead as will the homework you and your committee have done on the needs and operating requirements of the station. Also of value will be your professionalism in responding to those needs.

Public service deals with matters of interest and of help to the general public and includes services offered to the community by Planned Parenthood, city immunization clinics, the public parks department, YMCA, Girl Scouts, senior citizens, and other volun-

teer groups. Somewhere in there, religion enters the picture. You may be asked to participate in or provide material for a program devoted particularly to public service. In such a case the church message would need to be religious in nature but not strictly in content. You must never consider public service time, or any TV time for that matter, except what is bought and paid for, as "sermon" time. The sermon must be by example, articulated through some life experience. If your church is involved in a worthwhile program that has not been recognized, you might do some research on it and pass it on to the station. They might include it in a roundup of such works presented as a public service feature. Or they might suggest a spot about the service.

Most stations offer time for a certain number of public service ID spots at no cost. You get 15 seconds of the name of your organization or the event you are sponsoring, a telephone number, all of which share the screen with the TV station's logo. A few lines of live copy will be read with the slide. "Support the Camp Fire Girls. Today's program for today's girl. Call XXXX XXXXX," the copy will say while the screen shows a logo of the Camp Fire Girls, the phone number, and the logo of the TV station. Though these may not be overwhelmingly impressive, the value of them is that they may be aired during prime time programming. It's like having a free ride in a Cadillac without having to buy one. If you provide the copy and art work on the logo you want reproduced, the station may make up the slide for you free or at very small cost. Or you can have a slide done by a local producer whose name and services appear in the yellow pages under Television. You could get help from a nearby university or even a high school with a strong audiovisual department. Doing it yourself might be a problem unless you are thoroughly knowledgeable. Better leave it to the experts. If you don't have a logo, you might design one or have it done and made available in different sizes for a variety of uses—on stationery, for brochures, outdoor signs, posters, advertising, and TV spots. The original art work and velox copies of several sizes should be on file for ready use.

Help in promoting via TV spots a particular church project such as a summer camp for retarded children might be available in a variety of places. One that comes immediately to mind is the large corporation interested in similar goals. Assistance from this quarter has been offered church-sponsored projects ranging from community litter clean-up campaigns to literacy programs for adults. Help might also be available from local non-profit organizations such as the YMCA, Cancer Society, Red Cross, or from a service organization such as Rotary or Chamber of Commerce. The key to obtaining such assistance lies in fitting the interests of the prospective aiding group with the substance of the project. The Lions Clubs are interested, for example, in projects concerning good eyesight. The XYZ Corporation may have a history of backing projects dealing with senior citizens. It is beneficial to have in the files information about local groups and businesses and what kinds of projects they favor. A list might also be kept of the ones contacted and their responses. This gives a useful picture of groundwork that has been accomplished, and it can be instrumental in saving time in future contact work. The help you receive may be in the form of special mailings, statement inserts, a segment of free commercial TV time, a series of free radio spots, sponsorship of a proposed program. Business community prospects you might consider asking are: large department store, bank, consumer-oriented business, a business with a major payroll in the community. A direct plea for help will require some knowledge of the project, who it will reach, the projected timetable for its several stages, its current financing.

A company under contract with an advertising agency may direct their experts to design a TV spot or mailer at no cost to the church. They may give the free time or space as well. They may do the mailing gratis. If some official of the company happens to be on your bishop's committee or board of elders, so much the better. He or she should be contacted in order to help plan and should be given an opportunity to volunteer the firm's services. It might also be fruitful to suggest sponsorship of a worthwhile program in the local market. There are many of these produced by denominations at the national level or through ecumenical or denominational radio-TV operations. The important thing is to have all the facts at hand regarding cost, tape availability, length and duration of program, an audience profile. The approach might be made by phone initially, and finally by presentation of a detailed letter. Copies of all such letters with comments should be a part of the contact file mentioned earlier.

One church, following this system, called this their "Good Samaritan File." In it were a wide range of support and aid possibilities for projects, with comments and contact names. This proved to be of vast help to new communication people stepping into the job. When making contact, it is always helpful to leave the door open for future alliances. "Would you like to hear from us on a future public service project?" "Would it be possible that we might work together in the future? If so, what approach do you suggest?" Notes on these findings could form a useful part of the file. All contacts should be dated so that the next person to be in charge will know how recent the information is. The full communications committee should review all contact file information from time to time.

What about worthwhile programs produced by denominations nationally? How can they be obtained for showing in a local community? First, you must have access to information about them. You might get such data from your denominational publication, through some active ecumenical body, or by corresponding directly with the national offices of your denomination or its radio-TV production center if there be one. Much of the placement work is done at the national level. Local publications may receive listings as to when and where the offerings will be aired. If your viewing area has been skipped, you might put in a request to be placed on the list. Write to your denominational headquarters. Offer to do any liaison work required. If the denominational publication serving your area does not carry information or listings of their programs, you might take this on as a communications committee project. Tell them of your interest. Ask for their help in getting good religious programming into your area. If a release regarding a program appears in a local denominational publication, or if you have received a mailing and there is no listing of it by the local TV station, you might contact the station. Have as much information in hand as possible about the program. Ask what you can do to get such programming into your viewing area. If several churches or even several denominations were to show interest, the chances would be good that the local station management would be sufficiently impressed by audience possibilities to schedule the offering. You may have to organize that interest.

American Lutheran, United Methodist, Roman Catholic, Southern Baptist, Episcopal, and many other denominations, as well as ecumenical groups, regularly prepare professional programs of broad audience appeal. Many are as well done as the best to be seen on commercial television, and they prove that religion can be packaged in a palatable and professional way. Everything ranging from Gospel music and cartoons to issues and answers has been packaged and is probably available at any given time. Information on what is available, obtained through the communications committee, perhaps in concert with other churches in the community, is the best "handle" by which good religious programming can be brought into the local scene. Working through the ministerial group in a community, if there be one, might make it relatively easy to ascertain what is available denominationally. Would an ecumenical group want to partici-

pate in an effort to get one good Christian program aired? This could pose considerable internal difficulty, for naturally enough each representative of a denomination might be inclined to think his group's material best. But for the good of all it would most certainly be worthwhile to arrive at a consensus.

One problem often encountered in trying to place professionally produced video tapes of a religious nature is the time slot offered by the local station. The same time may not be designated week after week, thus making it extremely difficult to build a loyal following. The time slot may be poor in terms of the obvious audience. Then there is always the possiblity that the station will give no air time at all. At that point, if you consider it to be unjustified, you have recourse to the plea that the airways belong to the public, that the FCC will want to hear about this at license renewal time, that the percentage of public service programming is miniscule. There are national publications devoted to telling the public what their rights to the airways are. They may help you in your private battle.

OTHER TV AVENUES

Most of what has been discussed to this point involves the commercial TV stations of a community. There remain other avenues: public broadcasting stations, all-religious stations, cable.

PBS Television

PBS, the public broadcasting system channel, is usually supported by local community gifts and foundation grants for programming. It may have a drive every year to seek local subscribership. The PBS station may have a higher percentage of total programming devoted to local offerings. These may be more creative, more experimental, than most local material shown on commercial TV. PBS station personnel may be more inclined to work with local groups and offer help. PBS affiliate stations may be more deeply and seriously interested in local issues in depth. They may do an entire series on a particular topic. They may do location film. Often their subjects are expressions of the public conscience—pollution, discrimination, inner-city problems, law and order, women's rights.

They may offer the greatest amount of bilingual programming in a particular area. A church, interested in reaching a non-English speaking minority, may offer to cooperate with a PBS affiliate. Citizen participation works both ways, because the PBS station will probably have an ongoing campaign to tap such sources for funds for continuing operation of the station. A study of their programming will reveal who they are and are not reaching in a particular community; i.e., they may be heavily involved in morning programming for small children (mostly network) but have nothing for teens. If you have an idea for filling this gap with a locally produced live program or a tape of your own, you might have an excellent chance of being accepted. There might be major issues the station is failing to deal with but that would, if called to their attention, be greeted with interest. Since many local PBS facilities are located on college campuses, there may be a greater air of genuine inquiry and creative research as compared to that exhibited by commercial stations. A church's offer to help in a PBS affiliate's fund drive or information campaign would be appreciated and could set up good ongoing relations.

Church-owned Television

Today organized religion is buying into the media on a greater and greater scale. In addition to church-owned magazines, there are now church-owned radio and television stations and even networks. Groups of churches get together, campaign to raise money to buy a VHF station to be devoted solely to religious broadcasting. An annual telethon may help support it. A TV network, operated by one denomination, may present a great variety of programming to reach all ages and sexes. Some such networks are actively involved in syndication, both to networks of their own persuasion or to those operated by other denominations. Some divide up programming between their laity, clergy, and parochial schools, often using a large portion of their network time for educational offerings designed for classroom use. Many aim at those specific minorities not now reached in depth by religious TV—women, teens, seniors. The fact that a good part of such material is on video tape makes wider use of it both uncomplicated and financially attractive. The church that gets the local time commitment has but to purchase the tapes from the network and offer them to the station.

The cost of independent TV station ownership by church adjudicatories, or even ecumenical church groups, is often sufficiently formidable as to put it out of the question. However, a Chicago-based Roman Catholic UHF network discovered that its rate of growth was so healthy and the results of its efforts so positive that most criticism against the initial $4 million investment evaporated by the second year of business. Though the cost is seen as high in time, money, and research, many church leaders believe the expense is worth the results—getting the Christian message to

non-Christians through the most modern communication system. The church, many feel, should no longer content itself with Sunday morning service broadcasts because most of those already interested are in church or at home watching it on TV. The marketplace is so much broader that the church has a very real responsibility to speak via the medium that does the most effective job and has the highest level of verisimilitude.

At any rate, the point is that churches are increasingly getting into media ministries and the results are favorable. Because of this interest, a great deal more material of better quality is being put into the mainstream where churches, not specifically involved in programming on their own, may avail themselves of tapes at reasonable cost.

Cable Television

Cable opens another exciting and reasonable possibility for promulgating the church's message.

Cable transmission began as a service to communities which were not served by conventional television or where such service had proved to be inadequate. Most frequently it was introduced in towns located just beyond metropolitan areas where conventional signals were poor in quality but where a recognized commercial market existed.

The basic difference between the two methods of transmission is wire (cable) versus air (radio waves). The coaxial cable, installed underground along municipal utility rights of way, is capable of carrying 30 or more different channels simultaneously over a controlled path, free from obstacles and protected from outside interference from CB, radio, electrical, and other devices. Because cable requires municipal rights of way for its transmission system, it must be awarded a franchise from the municipality. Thus voters of a community have a say in whether or not their community will have such a system and to whom the franchise will be granted. Often the race for it gets quite hot with a number of interests vying for the franchise. Major political campaigns may be mounted to attract the voters' allegiance. The voter has as much a duty to study the ramifications of the different proposals as he has to vote intelligently on his mayor and councilmen.

Cable brings into a community not only better television reception but a greater range of viewing potential, including such heretofore precluded offerings as high school sports, stock market quotations, local community programs. Cable in a community can make impressive changes, affecting local politics, and enabling nonprofit, public service oriented groups to do a better job in communicating their work. Other services made possible by cable are two-way transmission situations where subscribers can transmit digital signals, voice, or video pictures back to the source of the programming and thus allow their input, reaction, and response to the original information. This is valuable in an instructive format such as might be used for service groups including hospitals, universities, and libraries. Cable viewers are able to register opinions on local issues. Being able to talk back to television puts this heretofore formidable electronic medium in a new perspective.

QUBE, a Warner Communications Company system in Columbus, Ohio, offers thirty channels with two way response buttons on home consoles. When a response is sought, the viewer will see the words "touch now" at the bottom of his or her screen. The options will appear immediately and the viewer will then touch the button that indicates preference. Opinion on local issues, lifestyles, material being viewed, consumer matters, is part of the input that can be transmitted through the console. Fire, burglar protection, and emergency ambulance service are among other capabilities of the system.

Cable differs from broadcast TV in that it provides, in addition to its local organization channel under control of the station management, a number of access channels including one public access channel for use by the general public; an educational access channel for use by public and parochial schools, as well as by libraries and other educational organizations; a municipal access channel for use by the local government; and a leased access channel which the operator can put to use on a commercial rental basis. Whether or not religion can get programming as public service on the local origination channel is largely up to the operator, many of whom shunt all such programming to the public access channel where the audience may be limited. Via the public access channel, churches can originate and produce their own shows and, develop their own audiences through promotion campaigns. Many cable companies allow free or low-cost use of studio facilities and equipment. The FCC stipulates that the cable operator must have minimum equipment and facilities for production purposes, including a studio, at least two cameras, and video tape recording equipment. Also basic lighting and a qualified adviser to offer assistance. Though most churches planning on cable use will need this array of equipment, there are some public access users who have their own equipment for video taping.

Cable differs from conventional television in that its revenue comes from monthly subscriber fees and channel leasing. Special events may carry with them extra fees as may educational courses and other cable services. The operator receives an initial hookup fee and monthly fees, as well as revenue from advertising. A major revenue potential is the transmission of first-run motion pictures to hotels and motels. Channel leasing to private groups for a wide variety of purposes is another source of income. Since the operator is dependent on local community support, he will be deeply interested in building public goodwill toward his operation; as a result, opportunities for the church in cable are quite good.

Who Controls Cable?

Cable is controlled by the FCC, by the wording of the franchise granted by the municipality and in a very large sense by the depth of concern of the citizens of the community. FCC regulations are directed toward the retention of channels for public use and toward the prohibition of certain types of materials such as obscenity, political announcements, and commercial advertising on the public access channels. Communications legislation concerning use of cable is still evolving and citizens might do well to inform themselves of the kinds of concerns being expressed by lawmakers at the municipal, state, and federal levels. The more interest responsible local groups show in using cable and protecting their rights to it, the more responsible cable operators will be.

How Can You Get Cable into Your Home Town?

There are a number of ways in which cable can be introduced into a community. The most obvious is when a commercial cable company deems the market sufficiently valuable to seek a franchise from the municipal government. Often these operators are part of a system known to the industry as Multiple Systems Operators (MSO) which means simply that one company owns a number of cable systems. A small number of MSOs at the present time own the largest number of cable systems in the United States. This may change as nonprofit groups and citizen-oriented bodies get into the competition for cable franchises. It would certainly behoove the public to be aware of whether an operator requesting a franchise in their town is a part of an MSO and what kind of service that group gives to other areas. Such data might influence a franchise vote decidedly.

In some cases the MSO may seek an alliance with a community group, finding it a beneficial way to get the necessary political backing to assure the franchise. The operator thus goes into partnership with the community group, which may represent a cross-section of interests of the community or perhaps one or two large nonprofit organizations. The community group would have to have access to some capital to make the venture possible. Selling stock in the company to local citizens may be one means of raising the necessary money.

The municipality may make a bond proposal to the community in order to finance its own ownership of the cable system. The municipality may elect to operate the system itself, operate it under a private management contract, or make an outright lease arrangement with a commercial operator.

A nonprofit organization may purchase a cable franchise. A church, university, or other such body may get together a citizen group of wide representation to participate financially. Capital can be raised through guaranteed loans, subsidized interest payment arrangements, or even through a foundation grant. A noncommercial group might contract with a private operator to run the system, keeping the ownership and policy-making functions to itself. In some cases subscribers own the system, pooling their capital, investing as little as $100 per subscriber in the initial venture, debt financing the balance. If the subscriber group opts to run the venture themselves, there may be problems of management conflict and too wide an interest range. Most such groups turn management over to commercial operators under management contracts. The review of operation and final authority on policy is reserved. The wider the diversity of interests represented by cable channel ownership, the more the public interest will be served. The essence of the present situation is that cable TV offers a service within the grasp of the ordinary private citizen, one which gives the public a surprising degree of participation in what is to be presented. There is probably no medium as sensitive to public opinion on a local basis as cable.

If you live in a town not now served by cable, you might want to institute an investigation of the possibilities. A good place to start would be a study of a cable operation in your general area. The facts about one operation could be incorporated into a presentation for your municipal authorities. A group of several churches of a single denomination, or an ecumenical group, would conceivably be able to spearhead an effort to obtain cable in a local situation. If your town now has a commercial cable operation that you feel is not sufficiently responsive to public needs, you might become involved in the formation of a public access board to rule on quality and use of facilities, scheduling and administering the public access channel. Such a group might be called on to raise funds for public access programming and for promotion. Information on forming such a group may be obtained from the National Cable Television Association,* or from Public Cable,* a nonprofit group of individuals and groups

interested in public involvement in cable. Some communities have put together cable TV advisory committees to inform the community about the meaning of cable for them and to do prefranchising opinion-gathering and other groundwork. This kind of approach also has the advantage of involving the community in cable before it arrives. Often a private citizen, either representing himself or a group, may receive appointment to an advisory board simply by writing a letter to the proper authority stating his interest and affiliation.

Cable: What's in It for My Church?
How Can I Use It?
Cable can be used to get specific tasks accomplished. A citizens' group in a large city wanted a piece of land in a poverty area developed as a public park. They made a video documentary about the problem and had it shown on the public access channel. A meeting of concerned people afterwards with the city council was also televised. Not only did they accomplish their objective but the entire community was made dramatically aware of the power of cable.

If there is sufficient interest and the public would be well served, churches can coordinate an effort to get a parochial school channel as a required aspect of a franchise between a city and the cable system. This was successfully done in one large southwestern city which had a number of Roman Catholic parochial schools. One channel was assigned for the exclusive use of the parochial schools in the city, and the resulting fare included workshops for teachers instructing them on how to use the televised material, an evaluation program for response to the programs, and an opportunity for input of teachers into content. The channel was also made available for use outside parochial school hours for others engaged in educational and community service activities.

In a north central city a group of churches formed an ecumenical group to produce a half-hour show on the local origination channel. The show was designed to encourage interest in the church's outreach. It offered parent effectiveness training, foster care programs, movie reviews, and discussions with well-known persons visiting the area. Some remote taping was done for man-on-the-street interviews on current topics.

Many types of cooperative ventures suggest themselves, from the church combining with educational and other nonprofit groups to take full responsibility for the programming on an access channel to the church providing some programming for the local origination channel using the cable operator's facilities as mandated by the FCC.

Leadership and responsibility for local program-

*See Appendix

ming are obvious needs when cable comes to town. Why shouldn't the church fill the gap?

A local cable operator will be more than willing to listen to your ideas for program provided you are willing to take over the bulk of responsibility and can assure him of your professionalism. When the glamour wears off, you are permanently stuck with schedules, writing, rehearsing, all the business of a full-fledged, technically demanding presentation.

From the beginning you will likely get a friendly reception from the cable people. If you are blocked from seeing them or get a turn-down, you have the alternative of referral to your city council representative of whom you can ask questions about the franchise. If you have a legitimate complaint, it will be heard. After all, the cable operation is where it is because you have helped put it there by your vote. In a word, they owe you. Cable is making money from your community, which is fine but at the same time the operators must provide the subscribers with more than just broadcast commercial programs or automated material. You have additional clout because you are able to deliver subscribers—your members who live in the area served. You also have the time to do advance promotion and to make an evaluation of audiences, both of which should be of interest to the commercial operator.

By using the medium the church acquires still another means of communicating with members and prospective members, of doing evangelism and of telling the Christian message in a living form. Television is a great motivator of youth; not only do they consume prodigious quantities of it but they are also excited by the possibilities of participating in it. Cable participation is therefore a good means whereby the interest of youth in the work of the church may be rekindled. Young people are intensely fascinated by visual media, they are thoroughly familiar with its power as a means of communication and appreciate the immediacy of its message.

Television production is capable of stimulating the interest of an entire congregation, young and old, in working together with merging of viewpoints and a new sense of responsibility for seriously presenting the Gospel beyond the church proper. Through participation in such a public communications medium, people begin to feel a new aspect of the power of being a church member and to discover a special delight in being able to manage what to a good part of the world must seem like an awesome responsibility. Spreading the Gospel seems essentially a here-and-now task when it is being done through the medium of the times. Furthermore, the prospects for sharing and having union with ecumenical bodies, with civic groups and educational organizations gives the Christian message another opportunity to be expressed outside the church, through personal interaction with all kinds of people and by striving with them toward a common goal. Church people can do their communicating task as Christians, forthrightly and unashamedly, something many of us find difficult to do in the ordinary course of events.

Some Opportunities for Cable Programming
The deaf television workshop is an excellent example of the use of cable facilities for a church-related effort. The program, "Deaf Digest," aired in Ontario, produced by the deaf and for the deaf, was supported by the Church of Canada. Out of it evolved the deaf advisory workshop which made itself available to travel and help other communities develop similar media work for the deaf. Many churches work with the deaf, and cable might be an interesting avenue for development of such a special ministry.

Many kinds of social works lend themselves to cable programming. Work with young children, with special children, with the elderly, with those who cannot read or write. A program of reading and music for hospitalized people was sponsored by a church which was intensely interested in that area of public welfare. The social work profile of the church can be catalogued and filmed for a magazine-type presentation which would lend itself to television. Such a presentation could say very clearly to the unchurched and to the general public: "All these threads, these works, are the church." The church would also be saying: "Christians care."

A church in the midwest produced a mid-week Sunday School for everybody under 18 and it turned out to be a delightful variety show, with emphasis on Bible lore, that was filmed in the church's own building. Music ministries lend themselves to TV, so do book and movie review programs (these can be five-minute segments taped in advance). Within your own church or the churches of your community there are probably a variety of possibilities for cable programming. You have but to look within for the material, brainstorm ideas with communications or different groups, to discover a wealth of material. The whole church could participate in the search for ideas. A call to the cable company could probably get you a resource person to sit in and listen to your ideas and help you work them out. Coupled with a knowledge of your own possibilities is the need for a knowledge of the local cable situation, how it works, what it needs, how you fit in.

A Bible school series produced on behalf of a local church coalition was aired in an Oklahoma city and subsequently won from the National Cable Television Association a local cable casting award.

Video tapes from a number of sources are available for rent or without charge for use by cable systems, to be returned prepaid after use. Such a one was offered by the Marble Collegiate Church in New York City. It included a series of worship services with Norman Vincent Peale preaching, all on one-inch tape. The programs were flexible in that they could be used in toto or as a sermon only (30 minutes). Check with denominational headquarters or ecumenical organizations in your city for video tapes available.

Don't feel that you are confronting the herculean task of producing only long programs. Consider five-minute segments such as book reviews, mini interviews, news briefs. Or single programs dealing with unusual events, introduction of an interesting person or group, close-up of a workshop, drama in rehearsal, art show, historical vignette (person, place, or building) or even a simple drama filmed outdoors or in a studio setting.

It can be interesting to brainstorm the possibilities. People get excited. The visual media have a fascination difficult to equal. Because of this it is necessary to keep the situation in perspective. TV—cable or broadcast—should be only one part of the overall communications effort. Seeing it as one facet of a larger effort, one which must be integrated with print and other media, keeps it from becoming an unrealistic ego trip for a few people. The love affair, if there be one, must be with content, not with the medium.

Because of the many changes in the electronic communications field it is difficult to give at any one time definitive data about hardware and methods. You have to keep your eyes on the changes by consulting magazines and books, by attending cable workshops, by interfacing with others in the commuity who are using cable and are aware of changes and ends. Some groups are working with satellite transmission which may well supersede cable. Small disc receivers will probably be available in the not too distant future, and the prospects are that they will be priced within reach of individuals. Until that time we must make use of what we have and concentrate on developing a media attitude that will be helpful regardless of what kinds of new equipment and mechanics are available. As children of God and followers of Christ we will continue to find joy in reaching out with our work, while at the same time viewing it as a serious duty of discipleship. We have a responsibility to be as courageous and as effective as possible, even when following unfamiliar paths.

Television: Using the Equipment

Many churches ask: "But can we use video tape ourselves? What does it involve? How about cost?"

Is videotape to be regarded a working tool within the grasp of the economically average congregation? Or is it an expensive luxury?

Because of the price (minimum of $2,000), VTR would have to be in the latter category for many churches. There simply is not that much money to spend on a device that (1) would be regarded by many as a play toy or ego-satisfying media trip for a few people, and (2) would have to be viewed as an expensive alternative to other approaches to the church's tasks of Christian education and communication.

Churches with large congregations, persuaded of their role in leadership, with highly developed departments of education and a deep interest in communication, already either use VTR in a variety of ways or are seriously considering it.

Smaller churches may not rule it out altogether. It is possible to rent what equipment you need: basically camera, tape deck, and monitor. Rental requires very tight working schedules and a high degree of organization of people involved so as to keep costs at a minimum.

Much of the good of using VTR will come internally by involving people in the process of seeing themselves in a new, authentic way. People who use it agree heartily that "there's nothing like it." Primarily VTR is a proven asset for a Department of Christian Education, both for teaching teachers and for use in classes. It offers outstanding capability for deepening self-knowledge and for developing formulae and techniques for self-criticism. Events taped and played back within the congregation can give a unique opportunity for all people of the church to know and understand what others are doing. VTR brings together as it involves. At the same time it offers opportunity for the participatory experience through avenues such as worship discussion, drama, or music. VTR can be a welding form between church and community. By working with citizens' groups to develop community programming and to focus public attention on community problems, the church can take its full role as a caring member of the community. Evangelism, ecumenical understanding, and intradenominational sharing are other benefits to be gained through VTR programs. Using its own VTR equipment, it can give the church a high degree of control over what it might offer to local cable TV. Because there remain some problems with technical quality and the need exists to transfer ½" VTR tape to broadcast tape, this would have to rank as one of the minor points in developing a rationale for acquiring and using a VTR system. Nevertheless, as expertise grows, this aspect could readily become a most important challenge.

Rental of equipment would be a wise way to determine whether or not the equipment satisfies a particular set of demands, whether it would be worthwhile to consider eventual purchase.

There are many ways to acquire the modicum of expertise necessary to use a system. The rental people will give you a short course. Local dealers in VTR systems welcome inquiries and are happy to set up demonstrations or give time to answer questions. Churches often find it agreeable to work with public high schools, many of which have VTR systems, or with universities or community nonprofit groups.

If you can use a tape recorder and a camera, you can use a VTR system. But you must think of what you are doing as taping rather than shooting film, a mental block that is difficult for many to overcome. Focusing is a matter of adjusting yourself visually to the mechanics of the camera and, since what you see is what you get, it poses no overwhelming problems. Forget about frames-per-second. The aperture is controlled automatically. A zoom lens gives you the possibility of creating interesting variety. In recording a literacy workshop, the camera operator zoomed from the group working to close-ups of mouths, helping students "see" the words being formed.

Getting the camera into action is a matter of focusing the picture you see on the screen, pressing and releasing the trigger which rolls the tape. If the camera is mounted directly on a tripod the handle with trigger will be set aside and the camera activated by pushing a button just below the lens. A red light on the camera shows that you are in record mode. You have the option of shooting all your tape time in one basic position—probably with the camera on a tripod—or of taking only a portion of the tape in this situation. If you are shooting a teacher's training session, you may want to leave the camera on the tripod with the lens focused to include whatever part of the scene you wish to record. You may wish to be in the picture yourself, which is easily accomplished in such a situation. Focus, push the record button, and join the crowd.

Variety can be obtained by zooming, changing props, moving position, recording at different distances, changing light. A distinct advantage over film is the instant viewing option. You simply rewind the tape as you would on an audio recorder, put the recorder in play mode and watch the picture on the viewfinder. To hear the audio, connect an earphone to the earphone jack. You can also play back through the monitor or a home TV set if you have the necessary adapter.

What about light, an essential element in any kind of picture taking? You have an F-stop ring on the portable camera. As you adjust it to the higher numbers, you automatically cut down the amount of light going through the lens, so this is the range you will want for bright light conditions. As you move it toward the lower range the lens is said to be open and more light is admitted. Also, the lens opening affects your focus. The further you are toward the higher numbers the more depth of field or range of sharpness you will have in your scene. The automatic gain control causes the amount of light to adjust automatically. However, light must still be taken into consideration by the operator. A medium contrast, evenly

lighted situation is best, but for drama a harsher degree of contrast may be preferable. You might even want some aspect of the scene backlighted momentarily. Generally speaking, it is not a good idea to switch rapidly from a very high contrast scene to a low contrast one. Some tape might then be over-exposed and some under. You need the lighting to be as uniform as possible throughout your tape.

Using the focusing ring of the zoom lens, you can move from close-up to wide angle to normal coverage. Focusing is more critical in the telephoto mode, so it is well to have the camera on a tripod when using it. For best focusing, center the camera on some clearly defined portion of the subject such as the eyes. Turn the ring until it is sharp. The depth of field is greater when focusing is on distant objects and decreases as you focus closer to the camera.

Audio and video are automatically synchronized when you pull the trigger to record. The audio, like the video, is equipped with automatic gain control.

When you have finished shooting you can rewind and see on the viewfinder what you have done. If you have made mistakes, taken some footage you don't need, what then? In film you would face a tedious and expensive editing project involving cutting and splicing. But you can run the tape to the point where you wish to scrub, set up a new situation and shoot that within the time frame necessary. The counter will give you the exact time frame within which you must shoot. Keep rewinding and checking until you have just what you want on every portion of the tape. It is a good idea to leave a short bit of early tape clear, so you can put in later what you want in the way of a title or introduction. You can do that later, after all the basic tape has been completed.

If you decide later that you want to dub different sound, as of a commentator, or if you wish to add sound, you can do it through the audio dubbing capability of the VTR unit. Since your tape only has one audio track, if you dub in new sound on that part, all previous live sound will be erased. To assure smooth audio continuity you might want to do all your recording on an audio recorder, then play it and record it in toto onto your VTR sound track.

Check the room in which you are shooting for its audio characteristics. If you have a live situation, you should hear an echo when you clap your hands smartly. Pretest your audio by trying a brief bit of recording and playing back through a monitor, if possible. Or try checking it out on a regular audio recorder and playing back. You can do certain things to modify the sound-carrying characteristics of a room, such as moving furniture, arranging people, drawing drapes.

A script. Should you have a detailed or working script or none at all? Again this depends on what you plan to shoot. Let's say it's 30 minutes worth of ½" tape. If you are going to do a teachers' training session, for example, it would be well to have things worked out in advance so as to get maximum benefit from tape time. You could do a run-through of a part of it. Decide what props you will use and have them handy. Since this tape is probably to be shown in your own church it can be informal. Think in terms of its being used over and over again as a permanent teachers' training tool. Don't date any more of it than you can help. The beauty of such a tape is that it frees personnel to do other jobs, it preserves the talent of people who may not be in the church a year from now, and it gives an instant training course for perhaps one or two people who come aboard later in the year. It can also be used to preserve a visitor's appearance on the training scene. Each time you use the tape, you save an honorarium.

If you are doing a communications tape about one segment of the church's life, either for the entire congregation or for some segment of the community, you will want to consider in advance what you want to do, perhaps write a script, at the least do a storyboard. The dialogue need not be written out unless this is a segment of a play or other type of formalized dramatic production.

The tape may be a profile of your church's life for Religion Week in your community. (You don't have one? Why not?) The various churches may want to trade tapes about themselves—an excellent way to get acquainted intradenominationally, ecumenically, or even interdenominationally. Not all Baptists in a community know what other Baptists are doing. What are the elements that will tell the story? Brainstorm it. Do you want to depict every activity or only representative ones? Highlights, reenactments of outstanding events, everyday church life? The sermon, the youth choir, the organist, someone greeting newcomers at the door? What is the outstanding quality of your church? Its overall friendliness? Its dedication to Christian education? Its outreach? Planning is a must. You should have a theme, some quality you want to transmit or some informational point of focus.

Many communicators make the mistake of being uneconomical in transmitting information, of trying to show everything. In this way they run the risk of losing cohesiveness or impact or both. You have to consider the simple message. You are standing with Charlie. You want to tell him about your church— one-to-one. What will you say? If it's "Hey, Charlie, we're a friendly bunch of people," maybe that's the VTR message you will want to portray. Whom do you want to reach with your message? Newcomers? The congregation as a whole? The community? Some special group not within the church? One church developed a program of taped segments from the life of every church in its community, arranging a sharing system so all who cared to could have a glimpse of the varied quality of religion at that time and in that place. It was a rich experience for those who made the tape and for those who viewed it. An offshoot of that particular project was loaning the tapes to the local high school for use in a class on religion. By using the tapes, the young people had an opportunity to compare and contrast the work, worship, and people of churches they had heretofore known only by name. This was an important contribution not only to the church's self-knowledge but to the education of the community.

If you yearn to do some tightly edited, professional quality taping, you might discuss ideas with your local cable operator for possible use on the public access channel. You could even try getting into broadcast TV via public service-community affairs programming. If they respond that your signal does not meet FCC standards, pursue the possibility of having your tape dubbed onto a 2" standard broadcast tape. There are other ways of using ½" tape for broadcast: it can be run through a studio monitor and videotaped through a studio camera or shown live. If the quality is good, it may survive this kind of once-removed viewing.

One of the problems most people have in using this medium is that its mystique evokes fear, awe, overexcitement. Some people may be so anxious to get their hands on equipment that they can't be pried away from it. The joy and value of the experience is that everyone have some camera opportunity.

Everybody should participate in every phase of the operation. Those who are fearful present another problem, but as soon as they understand the ease with which a tape can be erased and "boo-boos" committed forever to limbo, they can usually be coaxed into participating. Having someone who is knowledgeable from outside or from your congregation do a live demonstration of camera operation is vastly helpful. The demonstration should include basic camera instructions, shooting, lighting, hook-up, maintenance, handling. It should include common probelms and how to solve them. Then, one by one, the people assembled should come forward, put their hands on the camera and go through the basic routine. Learning by doing is far better than learning by listening, though there must be some of both. The main problem is dispersing the air of mysticism that surrounds VTR. It's an ordinary communication system. You can use it.

If you see that VTR is going to be in permanent use in your church, you might consider setting up a skills laboratory with rotation of people in each skill. Everyone should be given a chance to serve as director, script person, camera operator, set handler, prompter, lighting director, sound editor, or whatever roles the production may call for. This works particularly well if a series of productions is to be done where there is abundant opportunity for the rotation system to reach all participants.

A storyboard, such as that used in film and in planning slides, can be helpful in planning a VTR production as well. It would have listing for the video shots and the audio, as well as rough sketches of the pictures to be taken. Putting the shots on cards makes the system easy to work with during production and creates yet another set of duties for the many willing workers you will have, hopefully, from the moment the project is announced. The storyboard editor will work with his group to rough out scenes and sound. To get the feel for such a cooperative effort it might be valuable to plan and work out from beginning to end a brief video segment of approximately five minutes, a microcosm of the larger production you plan to do eventually. By doing this you will help people develop a feel for their roles, and guide them into the best patterns for interacting. You could also have a group known as troubleshooters who know the pitfalls, particularly of mechanics, and how to overcome them. If the lighting is not right, or the sound needs beefing up, they can come into the project with remedial action.

Carrying the camera with you into the field is not a major problem. The portable unit weighs around 25 pounds, and if you have ever done any kind of photography, you probably won't be dismayed by its bulk or weight. It is fascinating to go out on the public street, into a downtown area or park with a portable equipment. Here is where you begin to feel that old media magic. People come in close, want to touch, ask dozens of questions. They may be amazed to learn that you are doing a church project. That often described as "moribund" institution may be "with it" after all. You may have an army of young people at the services next week.

Absorbing the cost of the video system may be difficult for small churches, and sharing may not be the answer since the mobility of populations makes arrangements difficult to keep tacked down. If you don't want to rent the equipment but wish to go for ownership, there are some possibilities for recouping the cost of the unit, perhaps with someone in the church on a profit-sharing basis:

1. Videotaping weddings. This practice is becoming more popular, particularly in large cities where more and more people are buying video tape decks to play through home sets.

2. Videotaping TV programs to order. You can charge the cost of the tape plus a service fee. Many people make a donation to the church as well. Before doing this you must familiarize yourself with copyright restrictions and the distinction between selling a tape and doing a service.

3. Videotaping activity in the church nursery or cry room. This may eliminate some baby-sitting costs.

4. Videotaping other personal events such as births, graduations, even funerals.

5. Renting out the equipment to responsible others. Get a damage deposit when you do.

6. Videotaping a program of note to be shown at a church function. This may be a viable alternative to having a live speaker. It is also a means whereby local churches can participate in hearing well-known religious leaders.

7. Sponsoring a do-it-yourself workshop, focusing either on a purely church concern (stewardship, Christian Education) that can be loaned out for a small fee to other churches, or on skill workshops of general interest that could be offered to other community groups such as scouts, women's groups, and service clubs.

Videotaping becomes more attractive as the routes for viewing proliferate. There are now available superscreens, larger-than-life TV systems equipped with 84-inch screens. More and more homes are coming equipped with viewing rooms to accommodate the new screening capability.

TV promises to permeate our lives more and more as sophisticated equipment continues to roll off the drawing boards. In the future are videodisc systems which produce programs on plastic discs for viewing on home sets. By means of simple switches on a compact home viewer and recorder, you can now tape a TV show on one channel while watching another. Other forays into the video-disc field are being made or are promised for the near future. The electronic messages on the discs are converted into pictures and sound by means of a sapphire stylus, or a laser beam. Pictures can be frozen for close study or motion can be slowed down to create unusual effects. Some discs have stereo sound capability. The players have jacks through which stereo speakers can be attached.

Lending libraries and mail order clubs for video tapes will quite likely outstrip the circulation of paperback novels and the Book of the Month Club in the fore-seeable future.

What all this says is that the age of television is here.

Those who learn how to use what is available as quickly as possible will be able to make the transition to the new developments as they arrive on the market.

HOW TO DETERMINE THE BEST MEDIUM TO USE

Medium	Advantages	Disadvantages
Print	Materials inexpensive (paper, ink). Production process simple & rapid. Distribution can be controlled. Long life, permanent referral possibilities. Subject can be dealt with in a variety of ways. Range of illustrative possibilities. Quick to complete, can be done by one person.	Static. May be hard to distribute. May be discarded before being read. Can easily be dull. Production doesn't involve many people.
Radio	Inexpensive to produce. Low cost and accessible receiving equipment. Relatively easy to get air time. Applicable for groups and individuals.	Needs quiet surroundings. No visual message. Hard to get cohesive public due to variety of listening habits. May only be heard marginally as people do other things while listening.
Film	Large audience potential. Color if desired. Equipment inexpensive and in good supply. Involves many people. Both audio and visual.	Expensive to produce and duplicate. Long time in production. Formal quality. No feedback. Hard to edit or change. Work can be dated.
Tape/Slide	Inexpensive to produce. Can be used with large group. Easily revised. Equipment available. Familiar medium. Involves many people.	More elaborate presentation may require tricky, expensive equipment. Audience tends to drift away. Audience easily distracted.
Broadcast TV	High quality. Large audience. Impressive authenticity. People relate readily to it.	Requires excessive time. Difficult to get into. Time is costly if paid for. Audience is often not one needed to be reached.
Video tape	Easy to learn/exciting medium. Inexpensive (compared to above). Tape is reusable, inexpensive. Instant playback. Portable equipment. Involves many people.	Only black-and-white is moderate in cost (color still prohibitive). Playback limited to small groups. Broadcast quality requires further investment.

CHAPTER FIFTEEN

Television: The Church as Consumer

A paramount question of our time concerns the role of the church vis-à-vis television as a shaping force of attitude and behavior. We are particularly concerned about the young. Is the church engaged in an unequal battle with television to prevail as the moral authority of the twentieth century? Is the score Lions 90, Christians 10?

Television is immediate, professional, authentic, and readily available to millions of Americans. TV makes many kinds of behavior, including sexual promiscuity and crime, seem not only OK but attractive. The criminal who holds up a bank, grabs the good-looking girl (who later falls for him) and drives like a maniac, leaving a swathe of pole-climbing cars behind him, may not be a bad act to follow. At the end, he is not even hurt, he flashes a wide grin and is assured by his lawyer that the charges may be dropped. If you see such a sequence often enough you may be ready to believe it. The fact that you go to church on Sunday may not be enough to offset what TV has been subtly doing to you all week.

What should the role of the church be in counteracting the pervasive influence of TV? Head-on combat? TV is no good, don't watch it? Censorship—only the good shall be shown? Should the church be oblivious? "TV is not all that bad, its influence is highly overrated!" Is there a third possibility, that the church can use television as a vessel containing Christian truth?

It is not only possible but highly desirable for the church to develop creative responses to the great national pastime. This is aside from direct use of the media through production of thoughtful material of its own. This is apart from the church's role as critic of that television which is violent, banal, or at severe odds with basic Christian teachings. There is a duty

here which we will discuss later on in the chapter. But the church can take the role of the participant in television by allowing ordinary commercial fare to be dissected, studied, evaluated, understood for both what it says and what it does not say. Its messages—direct and indirect—must be unmasked, its strengths and weaknesses recognized.

The church has the perfect mechanism for studying TV in its Department of Christian Education or Sunday School program. Studying television in the Christian context could form a viable segment of the year's calendar and could be done on every level with all ages concentrating on a program or series simultaneously, sharing observations with one another. Or the study could be made by each age level studying different aspects of programming.

A church we contacted indicated it was crossing over age barriers by having the young people take on an adult series and the older people study some Saturday morning children's fare. The course was related to how people treated one another in what was viewed. Some particularly interesting information on expectations emerged, some of which was used throughout the year as sermon material. At a general gathering the whole church was treated to a cross-play of ideas arrived at through the program. "We struck some useful chords, developed some new awareness about all kinds of programming," the Christian Education director commented.

All television, the wheat and the chaff, would be fodder for such a program. Commercials, soap operas, novels of the air, movies, educational programs, and news analyses are raw material that can be utilized to advance understanding of the human condition.

Most people are apt to become fairly eloquent about

the contents of a show they favor. They know, basically, what the characters look like, what experiences they had, who prevailed during the half-hour or hour they elected to watch. Beyond that their knowledge is apt to be sketchy. What kind of person was X? What options did he or she have in the particular emergency situation of the script? What motivations can you see for the action? Asking these questions might elicit a gruff, "Wadda you mean?" Most people can't be bothered; yet they spend an enormous part of their time taking in material about which they understand only the bare minimum. There is worth in almost all television but the viewer has to have the tools in order to dig for it. Admittedly, he has to expend a certain amount of effort. If he is involved in a group process where others are doing the same thing, it takes on the quality of an adventure.

A study of television can be inserted as a block within the Christian Education calendar several times during the year. Or it could be introduced as a special mid-week night or Sunday evening course for those wanting to participate. Here is a substitute for conversational interaction, the lack of which so many adult Americans deplore today. Offer a milieu in which they can sit around comfortably and informally to talk about "The Christian values of soap opera" or "cop shows, and 'sit coms' are dangerous to your Christian health." You can put up anything you wish on the marquee.

The group can meet to prepare what it will view and discuss, and what overhead questions it would like to address itself to. Questions about the main characters, the plot, the conclusion, alternatives, the violence. It would be interesting for members to give a brief critique of what they have seen for comparison. It might be helpful to rate the work on a pre-set scale with a point system agreed upon by the group. Not everyone in the group need be considering the program from the same angle, though sometimes it might be interesting to do this. Different segments of the group might consider special points, or each individual might have a different guide for reporting. Typical questions to be considered might be:

1. Did you see any biblical figures in the story? Did patterns?
2. Did the program reinforce constructive character patterns:
3. What role did destructive forces play?
4. What was the strength of the program?
5. How did the problem-solving in the program set up Christian principles?
6. Did the program raise unrealistic expectations for the character? For the viewer? How?

7. With what character did you personally identify? Why?
8. Was there any relationship between physical appearance, dress, or character with his or her action?
9. Did the program show only weaknesses without remedy?
10. Was anyone transformed? Did anyone grow? How does this growth or transformation relate to the Gospel?
11. How would this program affect young people from your household? From an ethnic minority? From an economically disadvantaged situation?

In addition to answering and discussing these questions, the group might wish to dramatize some segment of the show as it would have been had it been in closer conformity with the teachings of the church. Rewriting the script to make a show better from a Christian point of view, makes for an interesting exercise. Individual responses to televised material tend to vary so widely that a collection of these would provide more than adequate material for one or several sessions.

A rating system could well emerge from the activities of the TV group. This would be useful not only for the group itself but it may also be helpful for the entire congregation. Anything that will bring people to a more acute awareness of what they are viewing must be an important part of the ministry of the church in the twentieth century. The results of the group's rating and evaluation can be posted in a prominent place in the church. A rating list can be included in church mailings. Such results can also be shared with other churches with some interesting cross-pollinization of viewpoints.

Concern for television might well be the subject matter of a year-long program for the whole church. The initial Sunday School study could spin off into a complex of specialized groups which are a permanent part of the church's life, or at least as permanent as television.

Additional approaches for the discussion groups include making and using videotapes of programs to be discussed and viewing them and discussing them as a group, making audio tapes of the sound track and running these prior to the group discussion. This helps people to revisualize the video. Discuss not only the text of the program but the action, setting, music, camera work, suitability of commercials. The program might be criticized from a standpoint of creative excellence. What was unique about the presentation? What about the individual acting? The script? Would you say this program made a contribution to American culture?

Further, the group could spend some time in the role of watchdogs, stressing demands for excellence in what is shown on local TV through correspondence with a program's sponsor, local station, producer, network, the FCC. If the program is good, commendation is in order. If it is harmful, particularly for young children, the church should be saying that clearly. It should be encouraging other community groups to support what is good on television and to condemn what is bad. One church group may also investigate what national organizations dedicated solely to improving the quality of TV may be doing, to join forces with them, or to help set up local chapters.

People are inclined to say with a certain amount of moral indignation, "I know TV is rotten but what can I do about it?" They are indifferent, or they may be afraid that anything they do will bring America's free press closer to censorship. But within the Body of Christ, there are things which can be done, such as learning to make careful and thorough judgments and influencing people of the larger community. Is there·a more important ministry in America today when more and more people are becoming alarmed about the power of the tube? The hours you may put in to inform yourself and work to upgrade your own and others' TV viewing standards could be the most important hours you ever spent. Yet they may be insignificant compared to those hours spent each week in Little League, lawn mowing, watching TV.

The fact that a high percentage of Americans view TV uncritically, almost without recall or response, is cause for alarm. These same Americans are spending a good part of their daily lives in a vacuum, one that, while it may not actively harm them, has a tendency to dull their sense of response. The fact that many of these supine people are under eighteen is even greater cause for concern.

But why aim solely at TV? What about books, pornographic magazines, violence depicted in the newspapers? Should not the church be equally concerned with these media? For the church as critic this is true. But books are not read in the total mental fog that grips many television viewers. It requires some effort to read a book. Because your mind has to function while reading, you will more likely make judgments concerning what you have read. You will not be stretched out letting wave after wave of information, good and bad, roll over you, making no response, not even the one you might like to make—that of getting up and turning the set off. There is something frightening about looking at an empty screen after so much has been paraded before you. It is like the moment in the empty theater when everyone has gone. It is not that hard to put a book aside. You often watch TV without making a conscious choice of what

you are seeing. Christians should step into this vacuum with the kind of help that will enable people to develop a selective sense about what they see.

In addition to evaluating and studying secular programming, the church has a responsibility to look into and be critical of its own use of broadcast time. How much of it is oversimplistic, designed to produce immediate returns in terms of members and money? How much of it does what it should do, showing religious involvement in daily life? How much of it is designed to produce "instant Christians" who tomorrow or next week have no continuity with what they espoused at 11 P.M. one Sunday night?

The nation's electronic ministers and evangelists spend millions each year to bring their messages to people, buying their air time on the basis of professional marketing studies or planning full-fledged campaigns, including coordination of several different media in a selected area. There have been efforts made from time to time to curb what has been called a cancerous growth of this type of marketed religion, particularly on educational television and FM radio. The charges include mindless money-raising, banal content, the same kind of tasteless hard sell used to push aftershave and deodorants. It is probable that as a result of continuing petitions and inquiries, FCC studies will be made for some time to come. Ownership by religious groups of multiple educational TV or FM radio frequencies in the same area is under close scrutiny. Such housecleaning could well catch quality church communications in the squeeze. It is up to organized religion to get its own house in order as well as to go about slaying secular TV's dragon of violence and other socially demoralizing contents.

The National Council of Churches has stated that it favors religious programming in the form of dramas, documentaries, and discussion programs that convey hard information and insights about religion and its goals, "rather than preaching homilies to multitudes of the already convinced and the long-ago converted."

Preaching at people, an NCC spokesman said, is not the goal of religious broadcasting, for it can better be done within the church setting or on a personal basis. The purpose of broadcasting is to reach those who can't be reached otherwise.

How much does hard sell put the church in the main stream? Media blitzes are used successfully to push all kinds of products. Why not the church? Because the church is not a soap powder. Not a deodorant. The church must be entered into through a process of conscious decision making. To help people get to that point in a way that will be meaningful and lasting should be the goal of the Christian communicator.

Much is being written about the effect of television, particularly its violence and the value system it es-

You have to get up early to catch most religious programming.

pouses, on children. At least one national group is concerned exclusively with trying to alert parents to the hazards of excessive viewing. Possible ammunition in the fight to improve the quality of children's TV viewing if not the quality of the TV itself, include more use of public television where programming tends to be more creative and of noncommercial content; writing letters to local stations and networks saying what you do and don't like; developing alternative sources of amusement in the child's life such as reading, games, hobbies. Parents are advised to talk about good programs with their youngsters, discussing why they are good, talking about the difference between make-believe and real life, and about violence and how problems can be solved nonviolently.

What Aspect of Television Viewing Should the Church Be Concerned About?

In "The Scary World of TV's Heavy Viewer," an article in *Psychology Today*, Gerbner and Gross discuss the fact that the clarity and simplicity of what is shown on TV makes real-life solutions to problems seem cumbersome and frustrating. The family goes from economic and social rock bottom to the top of the ladder when mother wins a contest, son rescues the baby of a millionaire, daughter is discovered by a Hollywood producer, father saves a crucial business contract and gets a promotion. The TV version of problem solving is easy, clean, quick. The perplexity of the viewer, particularly the young, as to why goals are so attainable on TV and so difficult in life is understandable. TV is authentic. The people look just like you and me. Why should my life be different? Obviously there needs to be more realness in TV programming than a soundtrack of rock music, mod clothing, the latest in slang, actors dressed like the people next door.

Passivity in the face of televised violence may be a far greater cause for concern than individual displays of aggression occasioned by viewing, the authors say. Television enables us to accept violence without indignation, a stance which is readily carried over into daily life. This then may be another aspect of the church's objection to the showing of great amounts of violence on the public media. If it dulls the moral sense of the general public it is producing an inherently harmful effect that can be significant for future generations as well as people now. If I am not outraged by TV violence, chances are my children will not be. The church should be ready to recognize and applaud programming that presents good results from living within a system of positive values.

A third problem for the general public raised by televised violence is that of shrinking personal freedoms. Television exploits fear as an overwhelming element of life. People become more afraid and demand more protection, asking for increased use of force by authority to secure what they deem to be their personal safety. Personal freedoms have a tendency to shrink through this insidious but powerful process. When freedoms diminish, all suffer. The church has a long history of being persecuted by overuse of authority. If we are at the dawn of a new such danger, it would behoove Christians to recognize it and help it to become recognized.

Churches can and should have their say about how the church or members of the clergy are depicted on television—usually as impossibly saintly folk or bumbling, fumbling, well-meaning but hopelessly inept characters of the cloth. Occasionally a priest or minister is depicted as a romantic refugee, fallen from grace, ready to face impossible physical challenges. He usually appears disheveled, unshaven, and is supposed to elicit sympathy while wallowing in the dregs. It is not often that one is allowed to see clergy in a real-life situation, as a pastor helping others or as a minister interceding in prayer.

Television has been blamed for many ills in American life, ranging from an increase in murder and other types of violent crime including juvenile atrocities, poor nutrition, and ill-placed sense of what is valuable, to rampant materialism. Medical journals have published articles identifying television violence as a cause of mental health problems. The medical profession has been asked to express its displeasure through the boycotting of products sold on programs devoted to violence or other activities deplored by their community.

A boycott, if mounted by a widely dispersed group with sufficient numbers, could most certainly have an effect, since the advertising dollar must be spent where direct remuneration in terms of increased sales will result. Churches can affect TV in their local areas by campaigns of writing letters and telephoning to the local station, by taking out advertisements in local newspapers, by appealing to other public bodies, including schools, service organizations, youth groups for help. The voice of the public expressed directly in a responsible fashion will have an effect on what is offered by television, perhaps not immediately but certainly over the long haul. The medium at every level is sensitive to public opinion. The FCC, its watchdog, can be appealed to, as stated earlier, particularly when the license of the offending station is up for renewal or when there are obvious and flagrant violations of the public's right to the air.

The more concerned the church becomes over what is offered on television and how to view as thoughtful, responsible Christians, the better prepared individuals will be to upgrade the quality of the medium and to understand and improve their own relationship to it.

A Quick Checklist of Things You Should Know about Station Operation:

1. Stations are licensed for a three-year period.
2. Four months prior to license expiration the station submits its application for renewal.
3. All licenses in one state expire at the same time.
4. Citizen objections may be filed any time prior to the expiration of the license or 90 days after an application has been filed.
5. The station's public record file must be available during business hours.
6. The FCC categorizes programming into eight main groups: agriculture, entertainment, news, public affairs, religion, instruction (education), sports, other.
7. Programming is either local, network, or recorded.
8. When a complaint is filed with the FCC and a station offers to remedy its deficiency, its proposed changes should be put into writing and filed with the FCC as an amendment to its renewal application.
9. Citizens can interact with the FCC any time, but it is more effective when done at the time of license renewal.
10. Letters to a station are effective; a petition bearing numbers of names is even better.
11. A broadcaster (prior to becoming licensed) is charged by the FCC with making an effort to know the community the station serves and to program for that community's tastes, needs, and desires.
12. If a station cannot find sponsors for nonprofit or minority programming, they are required to offer it on a sustaining basis without commercial sponsorship. Requirements as to how much time of this nature must be given are not specified. The needs of the community and the public concern would be a factor in the amount of such programming offered.
13. The fairness doctrine that has been defined by the courts calls for responsible presentation of controversial issues.

Some Questions You Might Want to Put to a Local Station about Its Programming

How much commercial time is the station carrying? It must be no more than 16 minutes per hour (normal), 18 minutes per hour 10% of the time, and 20 minutes per hour 10% of the time during periods of heavy political advertising. In radio: 18 minutes per hour (normal), 20 minutes per hour not more than 10% of the time, and 22 minutes per hour not more than 10% of the time during heavy political advertising periods.

How does the amount of time promised by the station in its license renewal application for, let us say, public affairs compare to the amount of time such material is actually offered? Answering this will require a knowledge of the renewal application terms and the station's weekly programming.

Does the station offer opportunity for (1) local self-expression, (2) development and use of local talent, (3) children's programming, (4) religious presentations, (5) educational material, (6) editorialization by licensees, (7) politics, (8) agricultural information, (9) news/weather/markets, (10) sports, (11) service to minorities, and (12) entertainment?

Note: These questions concern the mechanics of programming. Questions of quality, taste, and other aspects of content may be legitimately posed by citizens groups.

Some Jobs for a TV Checking Committee:

1. Study the TV situation in your community generally. What is offered in the basic categories set out by the FCC? Use the *TV Guides* or the newspaper's listings to make determinations.
2. Study prime time and other time segments; particularly note when religious programming is offered.
3. Assign people to check out specific programs for quality. Have them render reports.
4. Get specific input on what the viewers feel is objectionable and what is good.
5. Draft recommendations for the committee to present to the local station or stations. If the situation calls for aggressive action, prepare a petition.
6. Communicate to the church the committee's feelings on programs of worth and on programs that might be harmful, particularly to children.
7. Draw up your own TV guide within the church of programs worth watching for the week. Post it on the bulletin board or include it in a mailing.

8. Prepare a study guide whereby a group could use televised material to accomplish an educational purpose. A series of guides keyed to the various Church School age levels could be prepared in conjunction with the Department of Christian Education or the Sunday School staff.

Appendix: Access to Information

RADIO/TV

North American Broadcast Section, World Association for Christian Communication, 600 Palms Building, Detroit, MI 48201 (newsletter, conferences, resources)

Episcopal Radio/TV Foundation, 3376 Peachtree Rd. NE, Atlanta, GA 30326 (tapes, study guides)

Catacomb Cassettes (see above)

Church Resource Systems, PO Box 990, Dallas, TX 75221 (United Methodist Communications Council; equipment, newsletter)

Multi Media Productions Inc., PO Box 1041, Virginia Beach, VA 23451 (training in videotape, workshops, consultation, discount video cassettes)

NCCC Chronicles, 475 Riverside Drive, Room 850, New York, NY 10027 (general news and information sheet including some AV/Communication reports)

American Baptist Communications, Valley Forge, PA 19481 (Communications conferences)

St. John's Community TV Center, PO Box 153, Knoxville, TN 37901 (church-owned TV station, training programs, consultants)

Media Action Research Center, 475 Riverside Drive, Suite 1370, New York, NY 10027 (Television Awareness Training)

National Council of Churches, Room 860, 475 Riverside Drive, New York, NY 10027 (film catalogues, cable, syndicated programs, spots, other resources)

United Church of Christ Office of Communication, 289 Park Avenue South, New York, NY 10010 (Parties in Interest by Shayon—a citizens guide to improving TV and radio; other materials covering the spectrum of church communication)

US Catholic Conference Office of Communication, 1011 First Avenue, New York, NY 10022

Jewish Theological Seminary Department of Radio and TV, Broadway and 122nd St., New York, NY 10027

Association of Regional Religious Communicators, 1100 West 42nd St., Indianapolis, IN 46208

Catholic Broadcasters Association 1027 Superior Ave, Room 630, Cleveland, OH 44114

National Religious Broadcasters, Box 2254, Morristown, NJ 07960

National Association of Broadcasters, 1771 N Street NW, Washington, DC 20036

Radio Adverstising Bureau, 555 Madison Ave., New York, NY 10022

TV Information Office, 705 Fifth Ave., New York, NY 10022

The Networks:
ABC, 1330 Avenue of the Americas, New York, NY 10019
NBC, Rockefeller Plaza, New York, NY 10020
CBS, Inc., 51 West 52nd St. New York, NY 10019

National Association of Educational Broadcasters, 1346 Connecticut Ave. NW, Washington, DC 20036

Chicago Archdiocese Multimedia Communications Center and Network, 1 Wacker Dr., Chicago, IL 60606

Paulist Productions, PO Box 1057, Pacific Palisades, CA 90272

Denver Community Video Center, 1400 Lafayette St., Denver CO 80218

Dept. of Technical Journalism, Colorado State University, Ft. Collins, CO 80523 (booklet: *A Community Television Production Experience*)

Educational Film Library Association, 17 W. 60th St., New York, NY 10023 (bibliography of resources in video and cable)

Blue Sky, PO Box 1773, Boulder, CO 80302 (cable workshops and videotape information)

Ecumedia, 475 Riverside Drive, Room 850, New York, NY 10027 (Audio Feed Service including tapes of religious news, available for yearly fee)

Publi-Cable, 1201 16th St. NW, Washington, DC 20036 (Conferences on Cable)

Federal Trade Commission, 6th and Pennsylvania Ave. NW, Washington DC 20590

Federal Communications Commission, 1919 M St. NW, Washington, DC 20554

Action for Children's Television, 46 Austin St., Newtonville, MA 02160

SW Baptist Theological Seminary, PO Box 22000, Ft. Worth Tex. 76122 (media center)

Committee on Children's TV, 1511 Masonic Ave., San Francisco, CA 94117

American Women in Radio and Television, 1321 Connecticut Ave. NW, Washington, DC 20036 (local chapters)

Center for Understanding Media, 75 Horatio St., New York, NY 10014 (compilation of information and experiences in schools using video)

Spectrum, the Billy Graham Program in Communications, Wheaton College, Wheaton, IL 60187 (magazine on Christianity and the media)

Religious Broadcasting Commission of Seattle, 212 Washington Plaza Hotel, Seattle, WA 98101

Interfaith Committee against Blasphemy, PO Box 90, Glendale, CA 91209

Publications and News Services (Radio/TV)

Teachers Guides to Television, Box 564, Lenox Hill Station, New York, NY 10021

Broadcasting, 1735 De Sales St. NW, Washington, DC 20036

Film Information, Box 500, Manhattanville Station, New York, NY 10027

Cultural Information Service, 74 Trinity Place, Suite 407, New York, NY 10006

Mass Media Newsletter, 2116 N. Charles St., Baltimore, MD 21218

Handbook for Publicity Chairmen, PR Dept., National Association of Broadcasters, 1771 N. St. NW, Washington, DC 20036

Petersen's Guide to Video Tape Recording, Petersen Publishing Co., 8490 Sunset Blvd., Los Angeles, CA 90069

Deaf Digest, c/o Grand River Cable, 48 Preston St., Ontario, CAN. (specialized use of cable)

Media Information, 475 Riverside Drive, Room 860, New York, NY 10027 (monthly newsletter)

The Videotape Book, Bantam Press, 666 Fifth Ave., New York, NY 10019 (paperback)

CASSETTES

Cassette Information Services, Box 17727, Foy Station, Los Angeles, CA 90057 (newsletter and directory)

Office of Communication, United Church of Christ, 289 Park Ave. South, New York, NY 10010 (information, booklets on all types of media including cassettes)

International Tape Association, World Tape Center, Tucson International Airport, Tucson, AZ 85734

Audio Text Cassettes, 8110 Webb Ave., North Hollywood, CA 91605 (catalogue) (Also Cassette Collectors Review—information and listings)

NEWSLETTERS AND COMMUNICATING THROUGH PRINT MEDIA

Shoddy Pad, a mini-communications manual aimed at those putting out church newsletters: Office of Communications Education, United Methodist Communications, 1525 McGavock St., Nashville, TN 37203 (they also offer free for stamped envelope a listing of companies offering artwork in both offset and precut stencils)

A Guide for Publicity Chairman: Consumer Relations, The Sperry & Hutchinson Co., 3003 East Kempner Rd., Cincinnati, OH 45241

So You've Been Elected Publicity Chairman (handbook), Occidental Life Insurance Co. of Calif., Occidental Center, Olive at 12th St. Los Angeles, CA 90015

Communications Notebook, National Center for Voluntary Action, 1785 Massachusetts Ave. NW, Washington, DC 20036

Promotion and Publicity for Churches, W. David Crockett, Morehouse-Barlow Co. (paperback, 1974)

Handbook on Church Public Relations, The Religious Public Relations Council, Inc., 475 Riverside Dr., New York, NY 10027 (1969)

Paste-Up, Rod Van Uchelen, Van Nostrand Reinhold Co. (a paperback handbook 1976)

All Church Press, Tribune Corner, Ft. Worth, TX
National Religious Press, 523 Ottawa Ave., Grand Rapids, MI
(both provide information on co-op printing)

Celebration, PO Box 281, Kansas City, MO 64141
MA Religious Designs, Inc., 1917 Xerxes Ave. North, Minneapolis, MN 55411
Logos Art Productions Inc., Wentworth Office Center, 33 East Wentworth Ave., West St. Paul, MN 55518
(all three are sources of paste-up art for church newsletters)

GENERAL

Audio-Visual and Super 8 Workshops, Marketing Education Center, Eastman Kodak Co., 343 State St., Rochester, NY 14650

VU Marketplace, 2 Corporate Park Dr., White Plains, NY 10604 (biweekly newsletter for users and producers of video hardware, programs, services)

United Methodist Communications, 1525 McGavock St., Nashville, TN 37203 (Clown, Mime & Puppet Ministry; also Media Workshops)

Video Systems, Intertec Publishing Co., 9221 Quivirs Rd., PO Box 12901, Overland Park, KS 66212 (monthly publication for those engaged in closed circuit communications)

National Audio Visual Assoc., 3150 Spring St., Fairfax, VA 22030 (annual convention and exhibit)

Practising Law Institute, 810 Seventh Avenue, New York, NY 10019 (information on copyright law)

Imero Fiorentine Associates Inc., 10 West 66th St., New York, NY 10023 (regional TV lighting and staging seminar workshops)

Association of Multi-Image, c/o Abington Associations, 947 Old York Rd., Abington, PA 19001 (national workshop on multi-image production)

Educational and Industrial Television, CS Tepfer Publishing Co., PO Box 565, Ridgefield, CT 06877 (monthly magazine; company also publishes ETV Newsletter, Cable libraries, Videoplay Report and Video Trade News; send for sample copies)

Training, the Magazine of Human Resources Development, Lakewood Publications Inc., 731 Hennepin Ave., Minneapolis, MN 55403 (monthly magazine)

Franciscan Communications Center, 1229 South Santee St., Los Angeles, CA 90015 (themed films and discussion format)

Previews, R.R. Bowker Co., 1180 Avenue of the Americas, New York, NY 10036 (Monthly Sept.-May; reviews 16 mm films, video–cassettes, slides, filmstrips, audio tapes)

The National Audio Visual Association has for a nominal price an audio-visual equipment directory that lists manufacturers of all types of equipment. Information on the directory can be obtained from NAVA, 3150 Spring St., Fairfax, VA 22031